//

AF758484

AMERICAN POLITICAL, ECONOMIC, AND SECURITY ISSUES

U.S. CIRCULATING COINS

INVENTORY MANAGEMENT AND DEMAND ANALYSES

AMERICAN POLITICAL, ECONOMIC, AND SECURITY ISSUES

Additional books in this series can be found on Nova's website under the Series tab.

Additional e-books in this series can be found on Nova's website under the e-book tab.

AMERICAN POLITICAL, ECONOMIC, AND SECURITY ISSUES

U.S. CIRCULATING COINS

INVENTORY MANAGEMENT AND DEMAND ANALYSES

CATHERINE SOLORIO
EDITOR

nova publishers
New York

Library of Congress Cataloging-in-Publication Data

ISBN: 978-1-63117-184-0

Published by Nova Science Publishers, Inc. † New York

CONTENTS

PREFACE

The Mint is the world's largest coin manufacturer. The men and women working for The Mint, manufacture and distribute circulating coins, precious metal and collectible coins, and national medals to meet the needs of the United States. This book focuses on coin inventory management, the Federal Reserve Banks, and the United States Mint.

Chapter 1 – Efficiently managing the circulating coin inventory helps ensure that enough coins are available to meet public demand while avoiding unnecessary production and storage costs. The Federal Reserve fulfills the coin demand of the nation's depository institutions (e.g., commercial banks and credit unions) by managing Reserve Bank inventory and ordering new coins from the U.S. Mint. GAO was asked to review this approach. This chapter examines (1) how the Federal Reserve manages the circulating coin inventory and the related costs, (2) the extent to which the Federal Reserve follows key practices in managing the circulating coin inventory, (3) actions taken to respond to potential changes in demand for coins and notes, and (4) actions taken with regard to the circulation of the $1 coin. GAO interviewed federal and foreign officials, experts, and industry representatives; reviewed documents and data on coin inventories; and compared the Federal Reserve's coin inventory management practices to key practices in supply chain management.

Chapter 2 – Federal Reserve Banks fulfill the coin demand of the nation's depository institutions—which include commercial banks, savings and loan associations, and credit unions—by ordering new coins from the U.S. Mint and managing coins held in inventory at the Reserve Banks and in coin terminals. Reliably estimating the demand for coins and efficiently managing the inventory of circulated coins is important to ensure that depository institutions have enough coins to meet the public's demand and to avoid unnecessary coin production costs. Since late 2006, rising metal prices have driven the costs of producing pennies and nickels above the face values of the coins. This chapter addresses (1) the Reserve Banks' process for ordering and distributing coins to the nation's depository institutions and (2) the extent to which this process meets depository institutions' demand for coins.

GAO interviewed officials responsible for coin distribution at each of the 12 Reserve Banks and met with representatives of 4 large operators of Federal Reserve coin terminals, 2 banking associations, the U.S. Mint, and the nation's largest coin recycling company. GAO also analyzed Reserve Bank data for fiscal years 1993 through 2007.

Federal Reserve and U.S. Mint officials generally agreed with GAO's findings in the chapter and provided technical comments, which were incorporated as appropriate.

Chapter 3 – This chapter is about the United States Mint at a Glance.

In: U.S. Circulating Coins
Editor: Catherine Solorio

ISBN: 978-1-63117-184-0

Chapter 1

U.S. CURRENCY: COIN INVENTORY MANAGEMENT NEEDS BETTER PERFORMANCE INFORMATION*

United States Government Accountability Office

WHY GAO DID THIS STUDY

Efficiently managing the circulating coin inventory helps ensure that enough coins are available to meet public demand while avoiding unnecessary production and storage costs. The Federal Reserve fulfills the coin demand of the nation's depository institutions (e.g., commercial banks and credit unions) by managing Reserve Bank inventory and ordering new coins from the U.S. Mint. GAO was asked to review this approach. This chapter examines (1) how the Federal Reserve manages the circulating coin inventory and the related costs, (2) the extent to which the Federal Reserve follows key practices in managing the circulating coin inventory, (3) actions taken to respond to potential changes in demand for coins and notes, and (4) actions taken with regard to the circulation of the $1 coin. GAO interviewed federal and foreign officials, experts, and industry representatives; reviewed documents and data on coin inventories; and compared the Federal Reserve's coin inventory management practices to key practices in supply chain management.

* This is an edited, reformatted and augmented version of a United States Government Accountability Office Publication, GAO-14-110, dated October 2013.

WHAT GAO RECOMMENDS

Among other things, the Federal Reserve should (1) develop a process to assess factors influencing coin operations costs and identify practices that could lead to cost-savings and (2) establish additional performance goals and metrics relevant to coin inventory management. The Federal Reserve generally agreed with the chapter's recommendations.

WHAT GAO FOUND

In 2009, the Federal Reserve centralized coin management across the 12 Reserve Banks, established national inventory targets to track and measure the coin inventory, and in 2011 established a contract with armored carriers that store Reserve Bank coins in their facilities. However, according to Federal Reserve data, from 2008 to 2012, total annual Reserve Bank coin management costs increased by 69 percent and at individual Reserve Banks increased at rates ranging from 36 percent to 116 percent. The Federal Reserve's current strategic plan calls for using financial resources efficiently and effectively and monitoring costs to improve cost-effectiveness. However, the agency does not monitor coin management costs by each Reserve Bank—instead focusing on combined national coin and note costs—thus missing potential opportunities to improve the cost-effectiveness of coin-related operations across Reserve Banks.

In managing the circulating coin inventory, the Federal Reserve followed two of five key practices GAO identified and partially followed three. For example, the Federal Reserve follows the key practice of collaboration because it has established multiple mechanisms for sharing information related to coin inventory management with partner entities. The Federal Reserve has developed some performance metrics in the form of upper and lower national coin inventory targets. However, it has not developed other goals or metrics related to coin supply-chain management. One key practice is for agencies to identify goals, establish performance metrics, and measure progress toward those goals. Establishing goals and metrics, such as those related to coin management costs, could aid the Federal Reserve in using information and resources to identify additional efficiencies.

To collect information on potential changes in the demand for currency (coins and notes), the Federal Reserve has conducted studies and outreach, including developing a long-term strategic framework beginning in 2010 to consider changes in demand and implications for operations. While the magnitude of potential changes in the demand for currency is inherently uncertain, the Federal Reserve anticipates a gradual decline in currency use, and officials reported such changes could likely be accommodated by the current system. While Federal Reserve studies and data indicate electronic payments have increased over time, currency usage has remained strong. For example, from 2009 to 2012, the value of currency in circulation rose about 26 percent.

Starting in 2007, the Federal Reserve took actions to overcome barriers to circulation of the $1 coin, such as holding regular meetings with depository institution representatives to gather feedback about demand for $1 coins. The Federal Reserve manages the $1 coin inventory as it does for all other coin denominations—overseeing distribution and ensuring sufficient supply is available to meet demand nationwide. Reserve Banks currently hold approximately $1.4 billion in $1 coins, an amount that, according to the Federal Reserve, is sufficient to meet demand for more than 40 years. Reserve Bank officials, depository institution representatives, and coin terminal operators stated that $1 coins are readily available to the public throughout the country, but there is very low public demand for these coins.

ABBREVIATIONS

BEP	Bureau of Engraving and Printing
COSO	Committee of Sponsoring Organizations of the Treadway Commission
CPO	Cash Product Office
GPRA	Government Performance and Results Act
GPRAMA	GPRA Modernization Act of 2010

October 28, 2013

Congressional Requesters:

Efficiently managing the nation's inventory of circulating coins helps to ensure that the coin supply meets the public's demand while avoiding unnecessary production and storage costs. Efficient inventory management includes anticipating changes in future demand for coins and notes—

collectively referred to as currency—in light of factors such as increased electronic payment options and changing economic conditions. The Federal Reserve System's 12 Federal Reserve Banks (Reserve Banks) fulfill the coin demand of the nation's depository institutions (e.g., commercial banks, federal savings associations, and credit unions) by managing coins held in inventory and ordering new coins from the United States Mint (U.S. Mint). In 2012, the U.S. Mint produced 9.1 billion coins. According to the Department of the Treasury (Treasury), coins worth approximately $42 billion were in circulation at the end of 2012. Reserve Banks hold a portion of these coins in storage, including approximately 1.4 billion in $1 coins.[1]

In 2009 the Reserve Banks implemented a new, centralized approach to the management of the circulating coin inventory. You asked us to review the Federal Reserve's management of the circulating coin inventory and future demand for coins and notes.[2]

This chapter addresses the following questions: (1) How does the Federal Reserve manage the circulating coin inventory and what are the coin management costs? (2) To what extent does the Federal Reserve follow key supply-chain management practices in managing the circulating coin inventory? (3) What actions has the Federal Reserve taken to respond to potential changes in demand for coins and notes? (4) What actions has the Federal Reserve taken with regard to the circulation of the $1 coin, and what more, if anything, could it do?

To address the first question, we reviewed documentation from and interviewed officials from the Federal Reserve and U.S. Mint. We also met with industry stakeholders (e.g., depository institution representatives and coin terminal operators) and academic experts to discuss their views on the management of the circulating coin inventory. To assess management operations related to the circulating coin inventory, we used the Federal Reserve's Strategic Framework 2012–2015 and the Committee of Sponsoring Organizations of the Treadway Commission's (COSO) Internal Control—Integrated Framework.[3]

In addition, from the Reserve Banks we obtained and analyzed coin inventory and production data from 2004 through 2012 and currency management cost data from 2008 through 2012. We took steps to assess the reliability of data used, such as interviewing knowledgeable agency officials, and determined that the data were sufficiently reliable for the purposes of this chapter.

To address the second question, we developed and validated criteria to assess the Reserve Banks' management of the circulating coin inventory with stakeholders' and experts' input. We worked with industry experts to identify a selection of key practices for supply chain management that are relevant to coin inventory management.[4] The five key practices we identified were collaboration, risk management, performance metrics, forecasting demand, and system optimization.[5]

Establishing, documenting, and following these practices is considered important to effective inventory management. For each of these key practices, we selected the individual supporting characteristics most relevant to coin inventory management. To understand the Federal Reserve's coin inventory management practices, we interviewed Federal Reserve and U.S. Mint officials and industry stakeholders. We then compared the Federal Reserve's coin-inventory management practices to the selected key supply-chain management practices. For each key practice, we assessed whether the Federal Reserve was following or substantially following the supporting characteristics (i.e., plans, policies, or processes have been developed and implemented properly for all or nearly all of the supporting characteristics), partially following (i.e., plans, policies, or processes have been developed and implemented properly for some of the supporting characteristics), or minimally or not following them (i.e., plans, policies, or processes are lacking for all or nearly all of the supporting characteristics). Thus, the individual assessments for each supporting characteristic served as the basis for the overall assessment for each key practice.

To address our third and fourth questions, we obtained perspectives on potential changes in coin and note demand, as well as the availability and use of $1 coins from officials from the Federal Reserve and U.S. Mint, and Bureau of Engraving and Printing (BEP) as well as industry stakeholders and academic experts.

In addition, we interviewed government officials in Australia, Austria, and Canada to obtain their perspectives on the leading practices in coin inventory management and potential changes in future coin and note demand. We selected these countries for illustrative purposes because they had replaced low denomination notes with coins and implemented coin-inventory management process improvements. These countries are not intended to be used for direct comparisons to the Federal Reserve's management of the circulating coin inventory. For more detailed information on our objectives, scope, and methodology, see appendix I.

We conducted this performance audit from March 2013 through October 2013 in accordance with generally accepted government auditing standards. Those standards require that we plan and perform the audit to obtain sufficient, appropriate evidence to provide a reasonable basis for our findings and conclusions based on our audit objectives. We believe that the evidence obtained provides a reasonable basis for our findings and conclusions based on our audit objectives.

BACKGROUND

Roles and Responsibilities

The Federal Reserve System is composed of an independent government agency—the Board of Governors (Board)—and 12 regional Reserve Banks, each of which is located in a Federal Reserve district. (See Figure 1.) The Board is responsible for maintaining the stability of financial markets, supervising financial institutions such as bank holding companies and the U.S. operations of foreign banking organizations, and supervising the operations of the Reserve Banks. Unlike the Board, the Reserve Banks are not federal agencies. Each Reserve Bank is a federally-chartered corporation with a board of directors.

Unlike federal agencies funded through congressional appropriations, the Board and Reserve Banks are self-funded entities that engage in a variety of activities that generate revenue, such as earnings from lending to financial institutions.[6] The Federal Reserve deducts its costs from these revenues and transfers the remaining amount to the General Fund of the U.S. Treasury (General Fund).[7] In 2012, the Federal Reserve transferred $88.4 billion to the General Fund. Federal Reserve revenues contribute to total U.S. government revenues, and therefore, if its costs can be reduced—such as through more efficient coin-inventory management— more of its revenue could potentially be contributed to the General Fund.

The Reserve Banks carry out a variety of functions for the Federal Reserve, including ensuring that coins and notes are available in quantities sufficient to meet the public's needs. The 12 Reserve Banks provide coins and notes to depository institutions, among other responsibilities. The Federal Reserve's Cash Product Office (CPO) manages the Reserve Banks' coin inventory from a national perspective, working closely with the Reserve Banks.

For example, CPO places monthly orders for new coins with the U.S. Mint on behalf of the Reserve Banks.

Other entities, including the U.S. Mint, coin terminal operators—armored carrier companies such as Brink's and Dunbar, that hold both Reserve Bank and other customers' coins in their facilities—and depository institutions play a role in issuing or managing the circulation and distribution of coins. (See Figure 2.)

For coins, the Treasury's U.S. Mint is the issuing authority. The U.S. Mint is financed through a revolving fund and generates revenue through various means including the sale of circulating coins at face value to the Reserve Banks.[8] Revenue in excess of costs— including all costs allocable to the U.S. Mint's circulating coin program—is transferred to the General Fund.[9] U.S. Mint facilities in Philadelphia and Denver produce and ship new coins for circulation to Reserve Bank offices and coin terminals. Approximately 170 coin terminals are operated by 15 armored carrier companies. Coin terminal operators receive deposits from and fulfill orders of coins for depository institutions on behalf of the Reserve Banks and other customers. As we have previously reported, coin terminals operate at no cost to the government because while they maintain Reserve Bank coin inventories at no charge, they earn revenue from other customers—depository institutions—from the coin transportation and wrapping services they provide.[10] Depository institutions order coins from the Reserve Banks—through an online ordering system called FedLine operated by the Reserve Banks—to meet retailers' and the public's demand; depository institutions' coin orders are fulfilled with new and circulated coins held at Reserve Bank offices or coin terminals. Depository institutions can deposit coins with Reserve Banks when they have more coins than needed to fulfill demand. Depository institutions contract with armored carriers to wrap and deliver the coins to them, ultimately providing these coins to retailers and the general public.

The circulating coin inventory consists of coins held by Reserve Banks—both in Reserve Bank offices and coin terminals—and those coins in general circulation for public use.[11] In 2012, Reserve Banks held about 5 percent ($2.1 billion) of the circulating coin inventory, and 95 percent ($42 billion) of the inventory was in general circulation. As of December 2012, the 28 Reserve Bank offices held about 50 percent of the Reserve Banks' total coin inventory of pennies, nickels, dimes, and quarters and about 92 percent of the Reserve Banks' total coin inventory of $1 coins. The 170 coin terminals held the remainder of the Reserve Bank's coin inventory.

Based on the Board's statutory authorities, it is responsible for note issuance, distribution, and processing.[12] For example, the Board is the issuing authority for notes and is also responsible for distributing and authenticating notes. The Treasury's BEP produces notes to meet the Board's annual note order. According to the Treasury, at the end of 2012, approximately $1.1 trillion in notes were in circulation and approximately $228 billion in notes were held by the Reserve Banks. In 2012, BEP production accounted for about 32 percent of the circulating note inventory. This is due, in part, to the amount of new notes that need to be replaced each year because they are worn or no longer fit for circulation. The Reserve Banks manage the note inventory through 28 note- processing centers and 10 note distribution locations. CPO also has a role in providing note services, including processing. Similar to the distribution process for coins, depository institutions order notes from the Reserve Banks through FedLine, and then place these notes in circulation to meet the demand of retailers and the public. The Federal Reserve also contracts with armored carriers to transport notes for circulation or storage. When notes are returned by depository institutions as deposits to the Reserve Banks, each note is processed to determine its quality and authenticity; coins do not undergo similar processing. During processing, worn and counterfeit notes are removed from circulation, and the rest are wrapped for storage or re-circulation.

$1 Coin

The Reserve Banks are responsible for ensuring the efficient distribution and circulation of coins, including the $1 coin, which co-circulates with the $1 note. Legislation has been introduced in Congress to eliminate the $1 note and replace it with the $1 coin.[13] In 2012, we reported that the federal government would receive $4.4 billion net benefits over 30 years if Congress decided to replace the $1 note with the $1 coin.[14] This most recent savings estimate is lower than the results of our previous similar analyses, in part, because the life of the $1 note has increased.[15] The Presidential $1 Coin Act of 2005 requires the Federal Reserve and the Secretary of the Treasury to assess and submit an annual report to the Congress on the obstacles to the efficient and timely circulation of $1 coins, among other things.[16] As we have previously found, while Congress sought to increase the circulation of the $1 coin in recent years, circulation has remained limited, in part, because the $1 note has remained in circulation.[17]

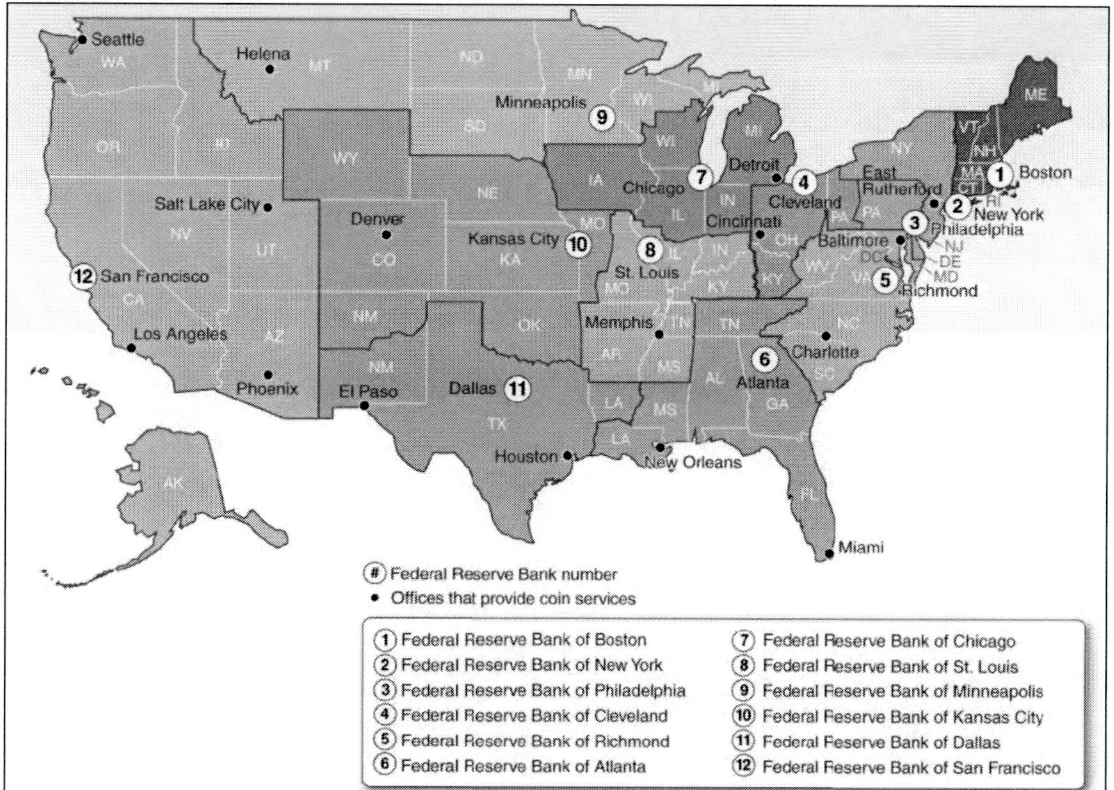

Source: Federal Reserve and GAO.

Figure 1. Map of Federal Reserve Bank Districts and Offices That Provide Coin Services.

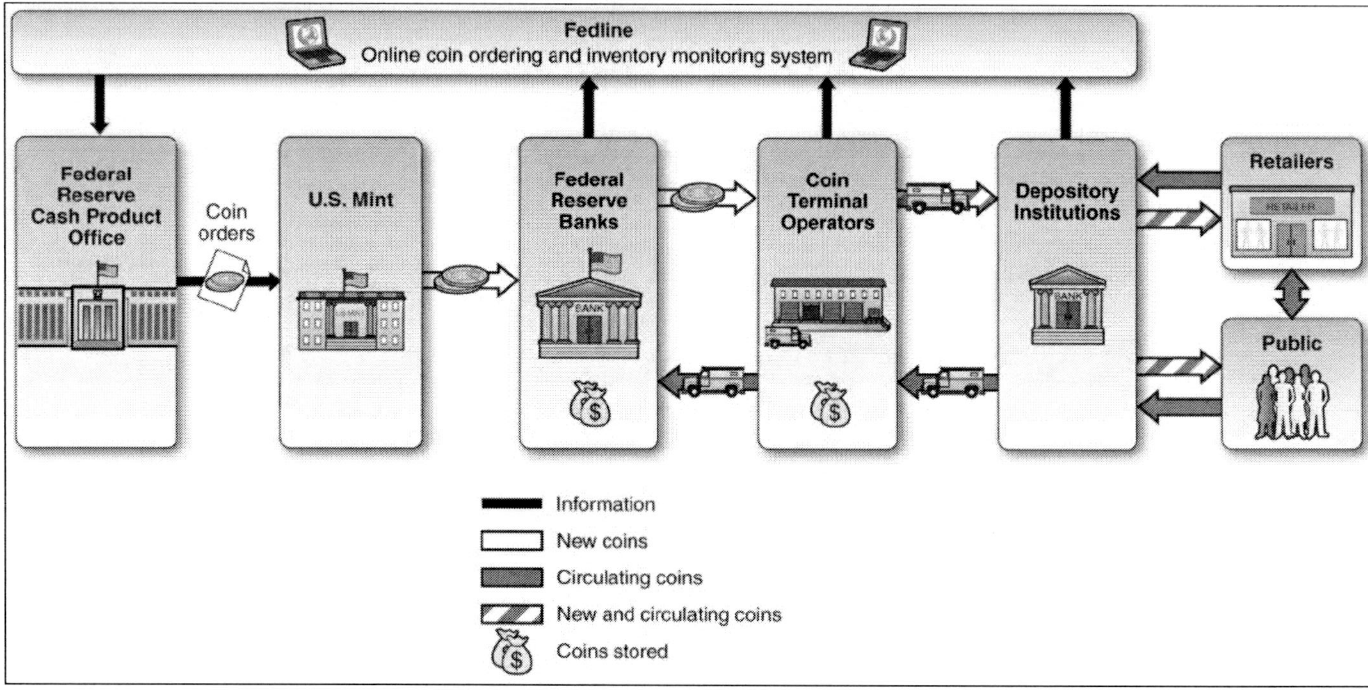

Source: GAO.

Figure 2. Production and Circulation of Coins.

Inventory Management Has been Centralized; Rising Costs Have Not been Analyzed

Coin Inventory Management

Since 2009, the Federal Reserve has made changes to its coin inventory management that includes centralizing the coin management system and establishing a contract with coin terminal operators.[18]

Centralized Coin Management

Introduced in 2009, the National Coin Inventory Management program centralized the management of the circulating coin inventory under the CPO so that the coin inventory would be consistently managed across the 12 Reserve Bank districts. Previously, each Reserve Bank office set and managed its own inventory levels, resulting in varying levels of inventory held relative to demand. Under the centralized approach, CPO manages the distribution of coin inventory, orders new coins, and acts on behalf of the Reserve Banks in working with stakeholders.

The centralized approach to coin inventory management was set up to increase the efficiency of the coin distribution process. Since 2009, Reserve Bank inventories for pennies, nickels, dimes, and quarters have decreased due in part to the centralized program. In particular, from 2008 through 2012, the combined inventory for pennies, nickels, dimes, and quarters decreased 43 percent.[19] (See Figure 3.) CPO officials have attributed these decreases in inventory and coin orders to the 2009 introduction of CPO management of the coin inventory but other factors may have also contributed to the decrease, such as the 2007–2009 financial crisis and recession, which may have affected the public's demand for coins.

As part of the centralized approach to inventory management, in 2009, CPO established national upper and lower inventory targets for pennies, nickels, dimes, and quarters to track and measure the coin inventory. CPO officials noted that these targets help meet their primary goal in managing the nation's coin inventory: ensuring a sufficient supply of all coin denominations to meet the public's demand. The upper national inventory target serves as a signal for CPO to reduce future coin orders from the U.S. Mint to avoid the risk of approaching coin-storage capacity limits and the lower national inventory target serves as a signal to CPO that there is a need to increase future coin orders to avoid shortages.[20] According to CPO officials, they view falling below the lower targets as more problematic than exceeding the higher targets because the lower targets are designed to guard against the more serious risk of not having enough coin to meet demand. We analyzed national inventory targets from 2009 to 2012 and found that in most cases the national inventory targets were met. However, inventory exceeded the upper inventory targets in 2009 for nickels and quarters; in 2010 for nickels, dimes, and quarters; and in 2011 for quarters.[21] In addition, the national inventory for pennies was 7 percent below the lower targets in 2012.[22] See appendix II for additional information on coin inventories, orders, and circulation.

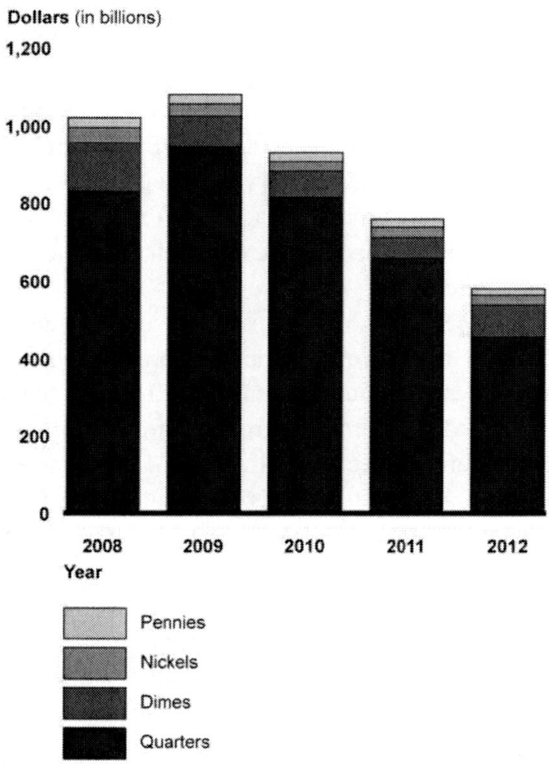

Source: GAO analysis of Federal Reserve data.

Figure 3. Reserve Bank Coin Inventory, 2008–2012.

In addition to considering nationwide coin inventory, CPO reviews the daily inventories of the 200 Reserve Bank offices and coin terminals and has established upper and lower inventory levels to ensure there is a sufficient but not an excessive supply of coins at each location. Given that the coin supply at each location differs depending on that location's typical volume of coin payments and receipts, each Reserve Bank office and coin terminal is required to hold a minimum 2 weeks of "payable days" and a maximum 3 weeks of payable days in inventory.[23] Prior to 2009, there were no required inventory levels for distribution locations and coin shortages and excesses occurred in specific locations.[24] Since CPO has centralized the management Reserve Banks' coin inventory, coin terminal operators we spoke with said coin shortages are less common and that they are better able to manage their inventory and provide depository institutions with the denominations they need to fulfill public demand.

In managing the coin inventory, CPO determines if coins should be transferred from an area with more coins than needed to fulfill current and future demand or if additional coins should be ordered from the U.S. Mint. (See Figure 4.) To make this determination, CPO uses a proprietary inventory management system that collects data on inventory, receipts, and payments from the approximately 200 coin distribution locations and forecasts expected changes in coin demand for each location. Before transferring coins from one region to another, CPO considers whether a region's future demand is expected to change and considers typical seasonal shifts in coin demand and local market factors such as coin- recycling operations that could affect the flow of coins. These transfers, known as interbank transfers, according to CPO officials, are the only direct coin transportation cost to Reserve Banks because armored carriers provide local coin transportation and delivery of new coins is provided by the U.S. Mint.[25]

Coins are also transferred between Reserve Bank offices and coin terminals within a region when distribution locations need additional coin supply or have excess coin inventory. For example, coins could be moved via interbank transfer from Reserve Bank offices in Seattle or Minneapolis to support distribution locations in Helena, Montana, and coins could be transferred among three distribution locations in Helena, a Reserve Bank of Minneapolis office, and two coin terminals. If there is an insufficient supply of coins to meet demand and transferring coins would not be cost effective, CPO orders new coins from the U.S. Mint.

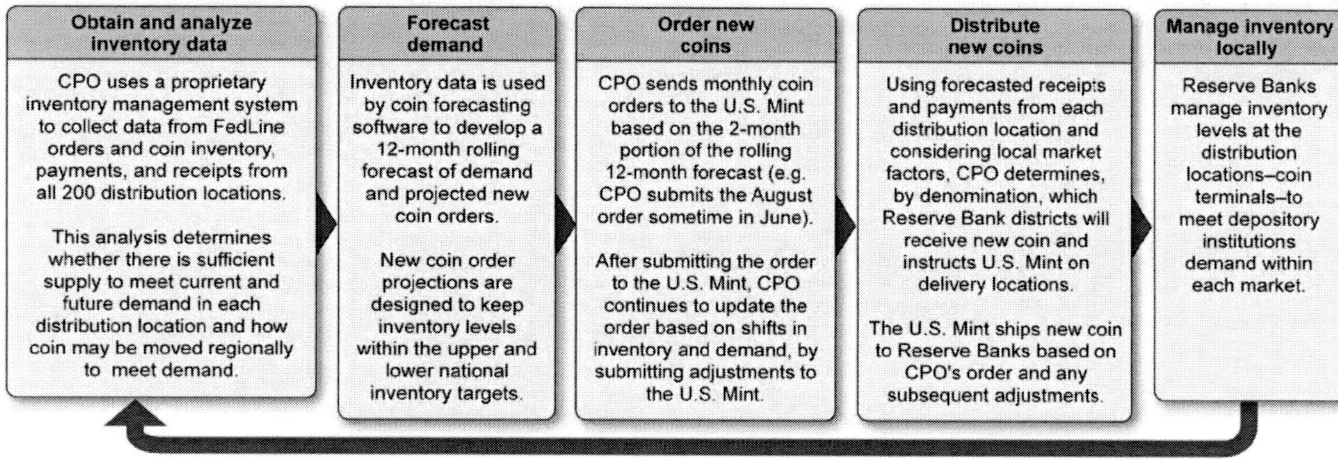

Source: GAO based on Federal Reserve information.

Figure 4. The CPO's Process for Developing Monthly Coin Orders.

CPO orders new coins each month from the U.S. Mint based on its 2-month rolling forecast of expected demand, as shown above in figure 4. CPO provides a monthly order to the U.S. Mint about 2 months prior to expected delivery (e.g., CPO submits the August order in June), and to help the U.S. Mint prepare for potential future orders, CPO provides estimates of projected demand and new coin orders for up to the next 12 months. After submitting orders to the U.S. Mint, CPO may increase an order or defer shipments to later months based on updated information. In part to respond to these changes, each month the U.S. Mint produces a safety stock of coins. If this stock is not applied to the current order, it is used to fill future orders.[26] After the new coins are produced, based on expected demand, CPO determines which Reserve Bank will receive new coins, and then Reserve Banks determine which offices and coin terminals will receive them. From 2008 to 2009, new coin orders for pennies, nickels, dimes, and quarters decreased by 79 percent; however, since 2010 new coin orders have increased annually.[27] (See Figure 5.) According to CPO officials, the 2009 introduction of centralized coin management led to the reduction in coin inventories and the more recent increases in coin orders reflect a return to a more normal ordering pattern that is closely aligned with payments to circulation and receipts from circulation. However, other factors may have also contributed to decreased new coin orders in 2009, such as the 2007-2009 financial crisis and recession, which may have affected the public's demand for coins.

Contract with Coin Terminal Operators

In 2011, on behalf of Reserve Banks, CPO developed and negotiated a contract with coin terminal operators, which standardized procedures and internal controls for the storage and handling of coins across all Reserve Bank districts. Prior to this contract, each Reserve Bank negotiated its own contract with coin terminal operators that operated in its district. We spoke with 5 of the 15 coin terminal operators, and they reported satisfaction and efficiency gains with the standardized contract and CPO's centralized management. For example, one coin terminal operator told us that the Federal Reserve's centralized approach allows coin terminal operators to manage their business proactively rather than reactively. Among other things, the contract requires coin terminals to use FedLine to order new coins and track changes to Reserve Bank coin inventory held by the coin terminal. Coin terminal operators have told us that FedLine works more effectively than the earlier ad-hoc communications to order coin and track inventory that preceded it.

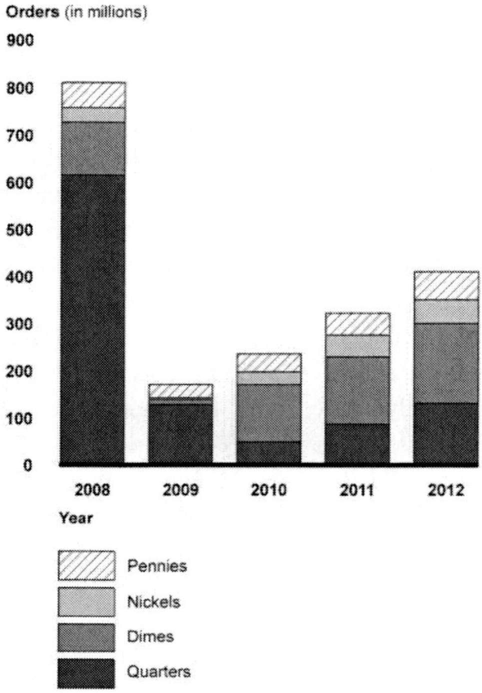

Source: GAO analysis of Federal Reserve data.

Figure 5. Value of New Coin Orders by Denomination, 2008–2012.

Coin Management Costs

In 2012, Reserve Bank costs related to coin management were about $62 million or 14 percent of the estimated $449 million that coins indirectly cost the U.S. government.[28] These costs included CPO's administration, coin handling, and interbank coin transfer costs.[29] The remaining 86 percent of U.S. government costs include about $387 million for the U.S. Mint's production and distribution of new coins. In addition, the government earns a return on the issuance of coins to the extent that production and distribution costs are less than the face value of the coins put into circulation—this value to the government is known as seigniorage. The U.S. Mint reported that in 2012 the government received about $106 million in seigniorage because the face value of coins produced was $493 million, and the U.S. Mint's cost of producing and distributing them was $387 million.[30]

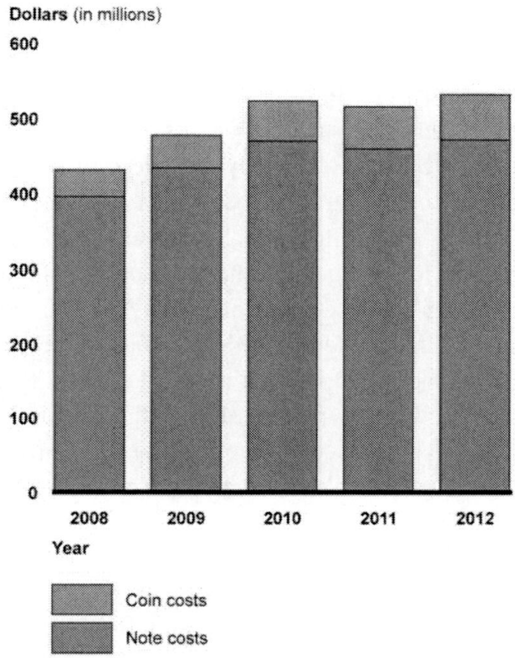

Source: GAO analysis of Federal Reserve data.

Figure 6. Reserve Bank Costs Related to Coin and Notes, 2008–2012.

The Federal Reserve's 2012–15 strategic plan includes an objective to use financial resources efficiently and effectively.[31] In addition, according to COSO, as part of the internal control process management should ensure that operations, such as managing an inventory, are efficient and cost effective, and this process includes monitoring costs and using this information to make operational adjustments.[32] To monitor costs related to coin and note operations, CPO officials said they review currency management costs—which include costs related to both coins and notes—at the national level because individual Reserve Banks may vary in their accounting for operational costs related to coins and notes.[33] When we reviewed currency management costs at the national level using data provided by CPO, we found that from 2008 through 2012 total annual Reserve Bank currency management costs increased by 23 percent.[34] (See Figure 6.) Cost information for coins and notes is available separately; however, CPO does not separately monitor coin costs.

Our analysis of coin management costs, using CPO data, indicates that coin management costs increased by 69 percent from 2008 through 2012. CPO officials attributed the increase in coin management costs to support costs, which increased by 80 percent during that time period, from $24.5 million in 2008 to $44.1 million in 2012.[35] (See Figure 18 in app. II.) Support costs include utilities, facilities, and information technology as well as other local and national support services such as CPO's services. According to CPO officials, support costs are influenced by a variety of factors, including the number and size of operating units at each location. Also, with the consolidation of some operating units, such as check processing, other operations, including coin management, have absorbed a higher percentage of support costs, according to these same officials. They further explained that direct costs—which include personnel and equipment—represent their primary measure of Reserve Bank coin operation costs. We found that direct costs for coin operations increased by 45 percent during this period; about $5 million across the 28 Reserve Bank offices. According to CPO officials, the increase in direct costs can be largely attributed to an increase in personnel costs, which may be influenced by volume of coin bags handled onsite and the number of coin terminals serviced.[36] By not separately monitoring coin costs, the Federal Reserve may be missing opportunities to assess and improve the cost-effectiveness of its coin operations.

In addition, we also reviewed coin management costs at each Reserve Bank and found that the rates of increasing coin-management costs differ across Reserve Banks. Using data provided by CPO on individual Reserve Banks' costs, we found that from 2008 through 2012, coin management costs increased for all Reserve Banks with the increases ranging from a low of 36 percent to a high of 116 percent.[37] To account for variations in the volume of coins handled by individual Reserve Banks, we also reviewed the average cost per bag handled by Reserve Banks and found that in 2012 it ranged from about $2 to $57 per coin bag.[38] CPO officials attributed variations in Reserve Bank coin management costs to different operational practices such as outsourcing coin handling to coin terminals and differences in direct and support costs.[39] While outsourcing coin handling may decrease some costs as personnel are not required at the Reserve Bank location to perform these services, it may also increase other costs related to daily management and periodic auditing of these outsourced services. Without taking steps to identify and share cost-effective coin management practices across Reserve Banks, the Federal Reserve may be missing opportunities to support more efficient and effective use of Reserve Bank resources. Moreover, more efficient management of the coin inventory may contribute to cost savings and additional funds returned to the General Fund.

The Federal Reserve Follows Some Key Practices in Managing the Circulating Coin Inventory but Lacks Performance Information for Additional Metrics and Forecasting

In managing the circulating coin inventory, we found that the Federal Reserve follows key practices for collaboration and risk management and partially follows key practices for performance metrics, forecasting demand, and system optimization. To effectively manage inventory, private and governmental organizations involved in production and distribution operations use supply-chain and operations-management practices. We identified five key supply-chain practices—collaboration, risk management, performance metrics, forecasting demand, and system optimization—and selected supporting characteristics applicable to coin inventory management to assess the Federal Reserve's management of the circulating coin inventory.[40] (See table 1.) These key supply-chain management practices are closely related, and improvements or shortfalls in one practice may contribute to improvements or shortfalls in another practice. In addition, establishing, documenting, and following these practices and their supporting characteristics contribute to a more effective inventory management system.

Key Practices Followed

Collaboration

The Federal Reserve follows the key practice of collaboration through its relationships with supply chain stakeholders, including Reserve Banks, coin terminal operators, depository institutions, and the U.S. Mint. CPO has developed policies and guidelines governing relationships with each of its partner entities. For example, as previously discussed, in 2011 CPO introduced a contract with coin terminal operators, which includes a manual of operations that standardized procedures and internal controls for handling Reserve Bank coins. CPO has also agreed upon roles and responsibilities with partner entities. For example, U.S. Mint officials told us that as part of the coin supply chain, they deal almost exclusively with CPO to manage day-to-day operations and interbank coin transfers. The U.S. Mint arranges coin transportation across Reserve Banks, and CPO reimburses the U.S. Mint for the cost of this transportation. CPO has multiple mechanisms, such as stakeholder working groups, for sharing information related to the circulating coin inventory with partner entities. Reserve Banks, coin terminal operators, depository institutions, and the U.S. Mint reported to us that they are generally satisfied with their relationships with CPO.

Table 1. Key Practices for Managing the Circulating Coin Inventory

Key practice	Definition and selected supporting characteristics	GAO assessment
Collaboration	Maintain working relationships with partner entities across the supply chain by establishing policies, roles and responsibilities, and mechanisms for sharing information. • Develop and use policies or guidelines governing relationships with partner entities. • Establish agreed upon roles and responsibilities with partner entities. • Develop and use mechanisms for sharing information related to the circulating coin inventory with partner entities.	●
Risk management	Plan and prepare for risks related to unanticipated events that could disrupt the normal flow of the system. • Identify sources of potential disruptions. • Assess the potential impact of the risk. • Develop and use plans to mitigate the risk.	●
Performance metrics	Establish, track, and reevaluate goals or metrics to measure change or improvement in a process or performance area. • Develop and use reasonable metrics that are clearly defined, measurable, actionable, relevant, and timely. • Track progress against those metrics or targets. • Establish and implement a process to reevaluate metrics or targets.	◐
Forecasting demand	Prepare for and estimate expected changes in future demand and plan and make decisions based on these estimates. • Have a process in place to forecast demand. • Use forecast results to plan and manage the circulating coin inventory. • Assess forecast accuracy.	◐
System optimization	Consider, as a whole, the strategic interactions and operations of the entire supply chain or inventory process in developing process change.	◐

Key practice	Definition and selected supporting characteristics	GAO assessment
	• Obtain access to information and resources from across the circulating coin supply chain. • Use information and resources to identify and implement efficiencies within the supply chain.	

● Key practice followed or substantially followed—plans, policies, or processes have been developed and implemented properly for all or nearly all of the supporting characteristics

◐ Key practice partially followed—plans, policies, or processes have been developed and implemented properly for some of the supporting characteristics

○ Key practice minimally or not followed—plans, policies, or processes are lacking for all or nearly all of the supporting characteristics

Source: GAO analysis of literature and Federal Reserve practices.

Risk Management

The Federal Reserve follows the key practice of risk management because it has identified sources of potential disruptions, assessed the potential impact of risk, and developed plans to mitigate risk at multiple levels of operations, including Reserve Bank, FedLine, and coin inventory management operations. For example, the lower national-inventory targets are set based on the highest consecutive 10-day gross pay period from 2009 to 2012 because, according to CPO officials, the U.S. Mint can produce and deliver new coins within 10 days. Therefore, the lower inventory target guards against a coin shortage if a disruption prevented circulating coin payments from depository institutions. In addition, risk management for the circulating coin inventory is built into the Federal Reserve's overall risk management and contingency protocols. For example, each Reserve Bank has a designated "buddy bank" to perform its functions—including coin circulation activities—if it is unable to operate due to a disruption. According to CPO officials, as soon as disruption is anticipated, they begin planning with stakeholders operating in the affected area, including Reserve Bank officials, coin terminal operators, and depository institutions. Continuity plans are also in place for Federal Reserve services such as FedLine. The FedLine website includes information on the types of potential disruptions, such as system outages or closures of Reserve Bank or coin terminal operations by inclement weather or other events, and what depository institutions and armored carriers should do in the event of a disruption.

Key Practices Partially Followed

Performance Metrics

The Federal Reserve partially follows the key practice of performance metrics because its use of performance metrics is limited to inventory targets and it has not developed other goals or metrics related to coin- supply chain management. CPO has established, tracks, and annually reevaluates performance metrics in the form of upper and lower inventory targets for pennies, nickels, dimes, and quarters. In addition, CPO closely monitors "net pay" to measure how well they are meeting general demand nationwide and at individual locations.[41] However, CPO has not established additional management goals or metrics to measure other aspects of its management such as costs because, as discussed earlier, CPO's primary goal is to ensure a sufficient supply of all coin denominations are available to meet the public's demand. Federal agencies have been required to develop performance goals and measure and report on their progress in achieving these goals since the Government Performance and Results Act (GPRA) was enacted in Although the Federal Reserve is not covered by GPRA, the Board has chosen to voluntarily comply with the spirit of the act. In addition, our previous work on managing results has shown that agencies should identify goals and establish a suite of performance metrics to determine whether they are meeting those goals.[43] We have identified customer satisfaction, efficiency, and costs, among others, as performance metrics that can be used to measure an agency's progress towards its goals.[44] Moreover, costs are among the common performance measures used in supply chain management. The Australian, Austrian, and Canadian mint and central bank officials we interviewed have established multiple performance goals and metrics for their coin inventory management.[45] For example, the Royal Australian Mint and its commercial bank partners have established targets to reduce coin holdings that will result in reducing the cost of freight and other related coin expenses. Further, the Royal Australian Mint tracks and monitors coin management costs to ensure that they are progressing towards their targets.

Forecasting Demand

We found that the Federal Reserve partially follows the key practice of forecasting demand because it forecasts future coin demand and uses this information to make decisions, but does not systematically track the accuracy of its monthly forecasts compared to the final coin orders. As discussed previously, CPO has a process in place to forecast demand by tracking current inventory, payments, and receipts and using this information to calculate expected future demand. These forecasts are then used to plan and manage the circulating coin inventory, including decisions on coin transfers and new orders. CPO officials told us they review their annual forecasts, and have found their forecasts for payments and receipts are within 10 percent of actual orders for pennies, nickels, dimes, and quarters. However, CPO has taken minimal steps to assess monthly forecast accuracy.[46] CPO officials told us that they compare their initial coin orders to net pay, but do not track the accuracy of their monthly forecasts because seasonal shifts in coin demand make reviewing annual trends more useful for their purposes.[47] Our analysis of initial monthly CPO coin orders and actual U.S. Mint coin shipments from 2009 through 2012 indicates that initial orders were consistently less than the final orders (i.e., U.S. Mint shipments of new coin). APICS—an operations management industry association that offers professional certifications—recommends that forecasting results must be continuously monitored and a mechanism should be in place to revise forecasting models as needed and that if the forecast consistently exhibits a bias, the forecast should be adjusted to match the actual demand.[48] According to the Logistics Management Institute, accurate forecasts result in effective and efficient inventories, whereas inaccurate forecasts often cause inventory excesses and shortfalls.[49] In addition, inventory management experts told us that accurate forecasts would make the Federal Reserve better able to respond to changing trends in coin demand, as discussed later in this chapter. Taking additional steps to assess forecast accuracy could help CPO identify the factors influencing forecast accuracy and then adjust forecasts to improve accuracy.

System Optimization

Although CPO has multiple systems that provide information from across the supply chain, we found that it partially follows the practice of system optimization because this information is not currently used to better understand some additional aspects of its coin management activities to optimize the efficiency of the circulating coin inventory. As discussed earlier, CPO has access to information and resources from across the circulating coin supply chain. This access includes information on actual and forecasted coin demand and Reserve Bank coin management costs, as well as information from stakeholders, such as new coin delivery information from the U.S. Mint. In addition, the Federal Reserve has taken some steps to identify areas where they could gain incremental efficiency improvements such as the centralized management of the coin inventory and note-processing efficiencies, which we discuss later.

However, CPO could improve its use of information and resources to identify and implement efficiencies within the supply chain by using the range of information available to establish and track performance metrics to measure progress. For example, the U.S. Mint's monthly production of new coins could be more efficient with improvements to the accuracy of initial new coin orders. Currently, the U.S. Mint produces a safety stock, in part, to ensure it is able to produce enough coins to fulfill CPO's final, adjusted order.[50] More accurate monthly forecasts and coin orders could lessen the need for the U.S. Mint to produce safety stock, and thus help to optimize the efficiency of the supply chain. In addition, if CPO used its information on Reserve Bank coin management costs and its knowledge of coin management operations across the 12 Reserve Banks, it could help to identify factors that have contributed to varying coin-management costs at individual Reserve Banks and opportunities for cost savings that could limit rising costs. Better information related to forecast accuracy and costs could also aid CPO in using its information and resources to identify inefficiencies and support system optimization. Further, optimizing U.S. Mint and individual Reserve Bank operations could potentially contribute to reducing U.S. Mint or Federal Reserve costs related to circulating coins, a reduction that could potentially increase the amount of money returned to the General Fund.

Demand for Currency Expected to Decline Gradually in the Near Term, but a Variety of Factors Make Predicting Longer-Term Change Difficult

Potential Changes in Demand for Currency

To collect data and information on potential changes in the demand for currency, the Federal Reserve has conducted studies and outreach with groups such as depository institutions and merchants, and found a general consensus that the use of currency may decline slightly in the near term. According to the Federal Reserve, this expectation is due, in part, to an increase in alternative payment options. Federal Reserve officials we met with described how interrelated factors make it difficult to predict long-term (i.e., 5 to 10 years) currency demand. The factors the Federal Reserve identified as influencing currency demand and the mechanisms used to supply that demand include the relative costs and benefits of currency versus other forms of payment, the level of economic activity and other economic conditions, technological change, and regulations and policies. Federal Reserve officials explained that how these factors will play out in the years ahead is unknown, and therefore the magnitude of the change in demand for currency is uncertain.

According to many agency officials, stakeholders, and foreign government officials we spoke to, while there may be changes in the use of various types of payments in the coming years, the effect on currency demand is likely a gradual decline. Thus far, Federal Reserve officials noted that their research indicates that the amount of currency in circulation continues to rise and currency usage is currently steady.[51] Federal Reserve studies and data also indicate electronic payment options have increased over time. For example, in a 2010 study, the Federal Reserve reported that the number of non-currency payments— including credit card and debit card payments, among others— increased 4.6 percent per year from 2006 to 2009.[52] Since 2006, the debit card has surpassed the check as the most used non-currency payment method, with the number of debit card transactions increasing 14.8 percent per year from 2006 to 2009. Over the same period, check volume decreased 7.1 percent per year. Many stakeholders noted that even with changes in non-currency payments, the effect on currency demand is likely to be gradual. For example, BEP officials stated that the increasing use of electronic payments has not had a major impact on demand for currency. Further, these officials said demand for currency may even increase and that growing use of electronic and mobile payments will likely affect checks more than currency. Royal Australian Mint officials also stated that while the use of electronic payment methods is expected to increase as new technologies emerge, how fast and when such a change will occur is unclear.

While data on credit card usage and electronic transactions are available, the volume of currency transactions is difficult to measure. Specifically, other data sources cannot be used to determine what portion of the currency in circulation is being used for transactions—for example, some currency in circulation are stored, as opposed to being deposited or used for commerce. As the use of non-currency payment methods has increased, the quantity of notes in the economy has also grown. According to Federal Reserve data, the number of transactional notes (i.e., $1s, $5s, $10s, and $20s) in circulation has increased steadily from approximately 19.6 billion pieces in 2009 to 21.8 billion pieces in 2012. During this period, the value of currency in circulation rose approximately 26 percent. (See Figure 7.) Coin terminal operators noted that there will be a continued need and demand for coins and notes, particularly because there will always be some portion of the population who will only use currency, such as individuals without bank accounts, or "the unbanked."

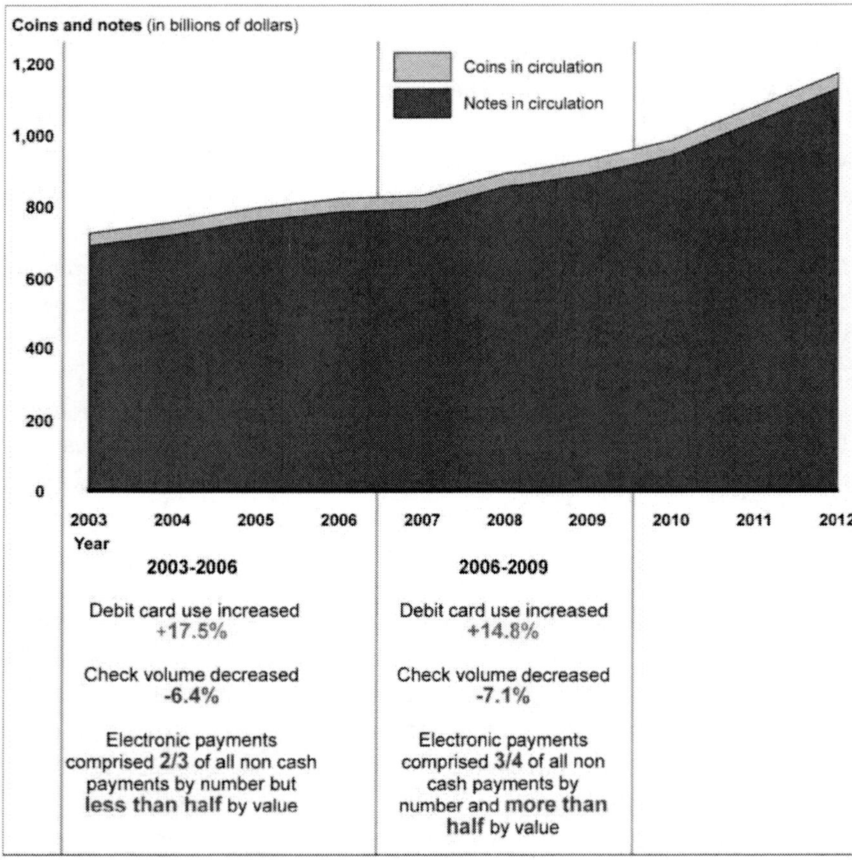

Source: GAO analysis of Treasury circulation estimates and 2007 and 2010 Federal Reserve Payments Study data.

Note: The Federal Reserve's 2013 Payments Study will include similar debit card, check volume, and electronic payment trends for the period from 2009-2012, but is not expected to be completed until late 2013.

Figure 7. Currency in Circulation and Examples of Changes in Non-Currency Payments.

Addressing Changes in Demand for Currency

Federal Reserve officials expect that their current procedures and approach to managing the coin and note inventory—including their forecasting and monitoring of the coin inventory targets discussed previously—will allow the agency to accommodate gradual shifts in demand. For example, to respond to increasing or decreasing demand for coins and notes, CPO can decrease or increase coin orders from the U.S. Mint and the Board can decrease or increase note orders from BEP.

Specifically, in 2012 the Federal Reserve assessed how notes received from circulation are processed and determined that current operations can handle a significant change in volume—either an increase or a decrease—without significant change to the operating model and staffing levels. Nonetheless, according to the officials, CPO is continually working to identify ways to streamline its processes to be more flexible and adaptable to changes. In addition, CPO and the Reserve Banks have established risk management plans and procedures to address the effects associated with a short-term, unexpected change in coin and note demand—such as from a natural disaster.

Other experts and foreign officials agree that well-managed currency systems are capable of handling major trend-based changes. According to inventory management experts we consulted, a key to effectively managing a supply chain is dependable forecasts. Effective forecasts would take both trends and cyclical demand changes into account. Therefore, combining forecasts with continual tracking of demand and inventory levels should allow the Federal Reserve to be able to adapt to any major trend-based changes in coin and note demand. As discussed earlier, this makes accurate forecasting by the Federal Reserve even more important. Royal Australian Mint officials also stated that by routinely monitoring activities such as coin trades and transfers between and among institutions, any changes in these or other measures would give officials insight on specific ways in which demand was changing, which would ultimately allow for adjustments in the volume of coins being circulated, responding to public demand.

While Federal Reserve officials we met with indicated their current processes should enable them to adapt to gradual changes in coin and note demand, a significant and unexpected change could affect the management of the coin and note inventories. According to Federal Reserve officials and some coin terminal operators we met with, the elimination of the $1 note for the $1 coin would be the type of event that could significantly affect demand for a specific coin denomination, and it would have implications for the overall management of both the coin and note inventory. For example, Federal Reserve officials stated that replacing the $1 note with the $1 coin would likely require increases in coin vault space and manpower as well as improvements in coin authentication technologies. CPO officials also said that if a large decline in coin usage occurs, they would adapt their management of the inventory in response. For example, if demand for coins were to decrease suddenly, leaving too many coins in circulation, the Federal Reserve would first stop ordering new coins from the U.S. Mint, and would then focus on storing the excess coin inventory. Coin attrition would reduce this inventory over time, and CPO officials anticipate that they would have sufficient storage capacity available to accommodate the excess coins. CPO officials told us that inventory levels would need to be well in excess of the existing targets before they would have an effect on storage capacity and related costs. Further, if public demand for coins decreased substantially, additional storage could be needed to accommodate and store the coins returned by depository institutions to the Reserve Banks. Coin terminal operators also did not expect a decrease in coin demand significant enough to exceed their storage capacity.

In 2010, CPO began to develop a long-term strategic framework to consider potential changes to currency demand over the next 5 to 10 years and how this change could affect CPO's operations. According to Federal Reserve officials, while the future is inherently uncertain, this framework is an internally focused effort to help them share information, refine internal operations, and monitor trends. The Federal Reserve has not established deadlines for completing this effort, but CPO officials said they continue to share what they are learning from data and other research, and they continue to assess current coin distribution and note- processing operations. The following activities are components of these efforts:

- *Engaging system stakeholders.* As an initial step, CPO officials interviewed stakeholders such as depository institutions, armored carriers, equipment vendors, merchants, and alternative payment providers to collect information and perspectives on potential changes in currency demand. Groups such as the Customer Advisory Council and the Cash Advisory Group also continue to serve as a mechanism for the CPO to coordinate and collect data and information on currency activity nationwide.
- *Examining internal operations for coin distribution and note processing.* CPO officials have sought to increase the efficiency of coin-distribution and note-processing operations to better position the

agency to adapt to future changes in demand. For example, the Federal Reserve enhanced its note sensor technology in 2010, improving the efficiency of note processing operations by nearly 10 percent, according to CPO officials. CPO officials told us that they continue to look for other areas to incrementally improve and add additional flexibility in their operations. Incremental improvements such as those related to note processing activities could contribute to supply-chain system optimization, as discussed earlier.

- *Conducting research.* The Federal Reserve continues to conduct research and analysis related to Reserve Bank operations. For example, one Reserve Bank is conducting the most recent in a series of triennial payment studies, which it expects to complete later this year, to determine the current volume and composition of electronic and check payments, reporting trends in these payments since 2009. As part of a broader effort to look at trends in various payment types, another Reserve Bank is examining the detailed spending habits of a selection of consumers, who were asked to document their transactions and payment decisions over a period of time in a shopping "diary." Because, as previously noted, determining how much of the currency in circulation is being used for transactions is difficult—this type of study can help officials better understand currency use in the United States. The diary study is expected to be completed and published later this year, and CPO officials told us they plan to assess and incorporate relevant findings into their currency management operations.

Australian, Austrian, and Canadian officials we interviewed are also exploring the potential impact of alternative payment technologies and continue to analyze past trends and to collect new data to inform these research efforts. For example, Austrian and Canadian officials have also conducted diary studies to better understand individuals' use of various payment options. Collecting detailed consumer payment information through these types of studies can help officials in these countries better understand consumers' payment and currency management habits.

The Federal Reserve Is Managing the Existing $1 Coin Inventory, Took Steps to Meet Demand for Circulation, and Plans No Future Action

Management of the $1 Coin Inventory

The Federal Reserve manages the $1 coin inventory as it does all other coin denominations, overseeing the distribution of coins produced by the U.S. Mint and those already in circulation.[53] The Federal Reserve's goal, based on its statutory responsibilities, is to ensure that sufficient supplies of coins are available to meet demand nationwide.[54] According to Federal Reserve officials, from an operational perspective, the Federal Reserve fills all orders it receives and treats all denominations of coins and notes the same.

Reserve Banks held approximately $1.4 billion in $1 coin inventory as of March 2013. According to the Federal Reserve's *2013 Annual Report to Congress*, this inventory level is sufficient to meet the demand for $1 coins for more than 40 years assuming a continuation of the current level of demand. Federal Reserve officials told us the annual net demand for $1 coins was approximately $51 million per year from 2010 through 2012. Inventory increased steadily with the issuance of the Presidential Coin series beginning in 2007, but has leveled off since the 2011 Treasury decision to cease production of new $1 coins for circulation (see Figure 8).[55] In addition, $1 coin payments to depository institutions have declined from $804 million in 2007 to $245 million in 2012, while receipts from depository institutions generally increased until 2012. In 2012, because there was less public demand for $1 coins than were in circulation, Reserve Banks received more $1 coins back than they paid out, as indicated by net pay in figure 8.

According to Reserve Bank officials, depository institution representatives, coin terminal operators, and vending machine industry representatives we met with, $1 coins are readily available to the public throughout the country. Most of the officials and representatives told us that they do not have problems obtaining $1 coins or supplying them to their customers, but emphasized that there is low public demand for these coins. For example, Reserve Bank officials in the Cash Advisory Group said that $1 coins are available at their locations nationwide and that they are able to fill customers' orders as needed. Depository institution representatives on the Customer Advisory Council told us their depository institutions routinely fill

$1 coin orders for organizations with standing orders—such as transit agencies or vending machine companies—but that requests from the general public are rare. A Federal Reserve coin terminal we visited also had an inventory of $1 coins, and officials there told us that while they generally receive $1 coin deposits, withdrawals are rare. In contrast, representatives from the Dollar Coin Alliance said that there is limited commercial and public access to the $1 coin and that some alliance members have had difficulty obtaining the coins from depository institutions. According to these representatives, the Federal Reserve's treatment of $1 coins—in particular, a limited ordering period for new $1 coins featuring a specific president—has hampered successful circulation.[56] However, other depository institution and industry representatives we met with did not identify similar access or availability issues.

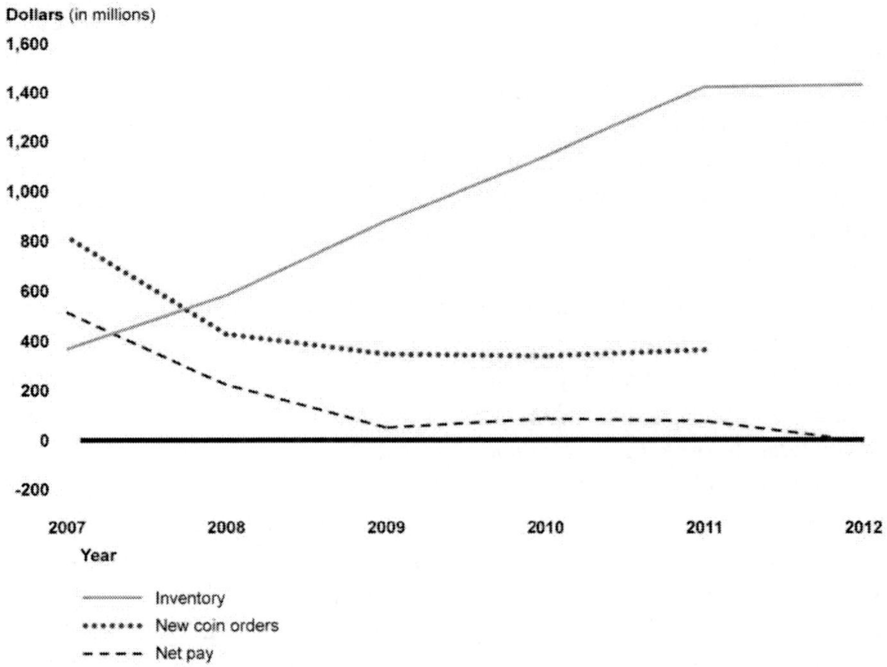

Source: GAO analysis of Federal Reserve data.

Note: Net pay is the difference between coin payments to depository institutions and coin receipts from depository institutions over a given period of time.

Figure 8. $1 Coin Inventory, Net Pay, and New Coin Orders, 2007–2012.

Federal Reserve Actions to Overcome Barriers to Circulation

Beginning in 2007, in response to a requirement in the Presidential $1 Coin Act of 2005, the Federal Reserve took steps to identify and overcome barriers to circulation of the $1 coin early in the Presidential $1 Coin program. The Presidential $1 Coin Act requires Treasury and the Federal Reserve to identify, analyze, and overcome barriers to the "robust circulation" of $1 coins, including improved methods of distribution and circulation, and improved public education and awareness campaigns.[57] Beginning in 2007, the Federal Reserve met regularly with depository institution representatives to gather feedback about demand for $1 coins and identify potential barriers to circulation. In its *2007 Annual Report to Congress on the Presidential $1 Coin Program*—a statutorily required annual report—the Federal Reserve outlined actions it had taken to eliminate identified barriers, including developing $1 coin distribution plans, establishing a special ordering period for new coins along with special packaging and order sizes, and communications with industry and other federal agencies.[58] In addition, the Federal Reserve and U.S. Mint conducted national and local outreach with coin user groups to gather input and help plan for the introduction of the new coins. According to Federal Reserve officials, most efforts began in 2007 and continued until the 2011 Treasury decision to cease production of the $1 coin for circulation.

While the Federal Reserve took steps to overcome barriers to the circulation of the $1 coin to meet existing demand, according to Federal Reserve officials, it can do little else given the $1 coin is no longer produced for circulation and the agency's statutory responsibilities focus on ensuring $1 coins are available to meet demand, not on taking steps to change demand. The Federal Reserve's *2007 Annual Report to Congress* reported that the U.S. Mint and stakeholder feedback identified the co-circulation of the $1 coin with the $1 note as the most significant barrier to improved circulation of the $1 coin. In addition, many depository institutions, coin terminal operators, experts, and foreign officials we met with identified the $1 note as a barrier to the increased circulation of the $1 coin and mentioned that eliminating the $1 note would increase demand for the $1 coin. However, neither the *2007 Annual Report* nor subsequent annual reports identified the $1 note as a barrier to the $1 coin. According to Federal Reserve Legal Division's attorneys, they do not consider the $1 note to be a barrier because they do not view co-circulation as limiting the circulation of the $1 coin. Rather, Federal Reserve officials noted the $1 note is an alternative to the $1 coin that the public freely chooses—that is, their view is that the $1 coin is fully available to the public and its circulation is thus at the level that the public demands. According to Federal Reserve officials, the Federal Reserve's authority does not extend to promotion, and therefore the agency is not likely to take unilateral action to promote wider circulation of the $1 coin. If this is the case, congressional actions would likely be the only feasible action that could replace the $1 note with the $1 coin.

Consistent with the actions of other countries, we have previously recommended that the Congress replace the $1 note with a $1 coin due to the financial benefit the government would receive from the replacement. As we found in our prior work, other countries that have replaced a low-denomination note with a coin, such as Canada and the United Kingdom, stopped producing the note.[59] Officials in these countries noted this step was essential to the success of their transition to the coin and that, with no alternative to the note, public resistance dissipated within a few years. Australian and Canadian Mint officials also explained that they took steps in advance of the issuance of their $1 coins to facilitate public adoption. For example, Royal Canadian Mint officials said that public outreach, stakeholder collaboration, and removing the $1 note from circulation were key elements of a successful transition to the $1 coin in Canada.

In its *2011 Annual Report to Congress*, the Federal Reserve stated that stakeholders and depository institution representatives reported through their routine meetings that the $1 coins continue to be easy to order and that its communications about the program have been effective, but that transactional demand for $1 coins has not increased since the start of the program and overall demand continues to come primarily from collectors. Federal Reserve officials told us they continue to discuss the $1 coin as necessary with groups such as the Customer Advisory Council, but that they do not intend to take any additional actions. The Board believes the suspension of the minting of the Presidential $1 coin for circulation makes the annual report no longer necessary and, in its *2012 Annual Report to Congress*, proposed the elimination of the annual reporting requirement.

CONCLUSION

Since 2009, on behalf of the Reserve Banks, the Federal Reserve has taken steps to standardize its management of the circulating coin inventory from a national perspective. Generally, these efforts have contributed to improvements, such as reductions in national coin inventories and orders, and stakeholder satisfaction with the Federal Reserve's new approach. The Federal Reserve's current strategic plan calls for the efficient and effective use of financial resources that could lead to more efficient operations and potentially cost savings. However, some issues remain.

- Reserve Bank coin management costs have risen since 2008 and CPO has not taken steps to systematically assess factors influencing direct and support costs related to coin management and assess whether opportunities exist to isolate elements of their coin inventory management that could lead to cost savings across the Reserve Banks.
- Interrelated key practices related to the Federal Reserve's management of the circulating coin inventory indicate opportunities to advance the use of performance information to establish and monitor additional performance goals and metrics and to improve processes for forecasting demand. For example, establishing goals and metrics and tracking progress toward those two will allow the Federal Reserve to better ensure that multiple aspects of its coin management activities are being monitored and will help agency officials identify and document other program impacts or to determine where additional efficiencies could be gained.
- Taking steps to assess monthly forecasts to improve accuracy can also lead to overall improvements in the coin supply chain. Developing and tracking performance information and assessing forecasts—key practices used by private and governmental organizations to effectively manage their inventories—could ultimately help identify cost savings for Reserve Banks or improve the efficiency of U.S. Mint coin production, which may in turn result in more money returned to the General Fund, contributing to U.S. taxpayer savings.

RECOMMENDATIONS FOR EXECUTIVE ACTION

To ensure efficient management of the circulating coin inventory, we recommend that the Board of Governors direct CPO to take the following three actions:

- develop a process to assess the factors that have influenced increasing coin operations costs and differences in costs across Reserve Banks and a process to use this information to identify practices that could lead to cost-savings;

- establish, document, and annually report to the Board performance goals and metrics for managing the circulating coin inventory, (e.g., Reserve Bank coin management costs) and measure performance towards those goals and metrics; and
- establish and implement a process to assess the accuracy of forecasts for new coin orders and revise the forecasts as needed.

AGENCY COMMENTS

We provided a draft of this chapter to the Chairman of the Board of Governors of the Federal Reserve System and the Secretary of the Treasury for review and comment. In written comments the Federal Reserve generally agreed with the chapter's recommendations. Treasury had no comments.

Lorelei St. James
Director, Physical Infrastructure

APPENDIX I. OBJECTIVES, SCOPE, AND METHODOLOGY

This chapter addresses the following questions: (1) How does the Federal Reserve manage the circulating coin inventory and what are the coin management costs? (2) To what extent does the Federal Reserve follow key supply-chain management practices in managing the circulating coin inventory? (3) What actions has the Federal Reserve taken to respond to potential changes in demand for coins and notes? (4) What actions has the Federal Reserve taken with regard to the circulation of the $1 coin, and what more, if anything, could it do?

To address these questions we met with federal agency officials, foreign officials, industry and academic experts, and currency industry representatives. (See table 2.) We selected industry and academic experts with supply-chain or coin-inventory management expertise. We selected Australia, Austria, and Canada as countries with experiences relevant to our review—such as replacing low denomination notes with coins, or recent implementation of coin-inventory management process improvements. These countries were selected for illustrative purposes and are not intended to be used as benchmarks for direct comparisons to the Federal Reserve's management of the circulating coin inventory. We obtained documents from and conducted interviews with Federal Reserve officials to obtain information about the agency's processes for managing the distribution of the circulating coin inventory. We also visited a Federal Reserve coin terminal in White Marsh, Maryland. In addition, we reviewed literature and our prior reports related to coin inventory management.

Table 2. Organizations and Individuals Interviewed

Federal agencies
Bureau of Engraving and Printing
Federal Reserve Banks' Cash Advisory Group
Federal Reserve Board
Federal Reserve Cash Product Office
Federal Reserve Retail Payments Office
United States Mint
Foreign officials
Department of Finance Canada
Oesterreichische Nationalbank
Royal Australian Mint
Royal Canadian Mint
Industry and academic experts
APICS
Dr. Dean Croushore, University of Richmond
Dr. Neil Geismar and Dr. Chelliah Sriskandarajah, Texas A&M University
Industry representatives
American Bankers Association
Coinstar
Customer Advisory Council
Dollar Coin Alliance
Independent Armored Car Operators Association
Independent Community Bankers of America
National Armored Car Association (Brink's, Dunbar Armored, Loomis)
National Automated Merchandising Association

Source: GAO.

To review the Federal Reserve's management of the circulating coin inventory and identify costs associated with managing this inventory, we interviewed Federal Reserve, United States Mint (U.S. Mint) officials, and industry representatives—such as National Armored Car Association members and depository institution representatives on the Cash Product Office's (CPO) Customer Advisory Council (a group established to provide input on coin and note operations). To assess management operations related to the circulating coin inventory, we used the Federal Reserve's Strategic Framework 2012-2015 and the Committee of Sponsoring Organizations of the Treadway Commission's (COSO) Internal Control—Integrated Framework.[60] We also obtained and analyzed coin inventory and production data for 2004 through 2012 from the Federal Reserve, U.S. Mint production data from 2010 through March 2013, and Reserve Bank coin and note management cost data from 2008 through 2012. For example, we reviewed Federal Reserve data for monthly coin forecasts, annual coin inventory levels, analyzed data on monthly coin orders and shipments for bias, and compared the overall and individual Reserve Bank costs related to coin and note operations.

To assess the extent to which the Federal Reserve follows key supply-chain and inventory-management practices, we developed and validated criteria with stakeholder and expert input. To develop and define practices common to efficient supply chain and inventory management and applicable to the circulating coin inventory in the United States, we reviewed supply chain management and operations management literature on leading practices, our past defense inventory management and Government Performance and Results Act reports, and academic literature.[61] We also worked with industry experts to identify a selection of supply-chain management practices relevant to coin inventory management. We identified five key practices: collaboration, risk management, performance metrics, forecasting demand, and system optimization. For additional information on these key practices, see appendix III. The supporting characteristics associated with the key practices were selected based on knowledge of circulating coin management. Selected academic and industry experts in operations and supply chain management and the circulating coin inventory as well as foreign mint or central bank officials from Australia, Austria, and Canada validated that the selected key practices, definitions, and supporting characteristics were relevant to coin inventory management.

We compared the Federal Reserve's inventory management practices to the five key practices by assessing the extent to which the Federal Reserve met individual supporting characteristics for each practice. The individual assessments for the supporting characteristics served as the basis for the overall assessment for each key practice. Specifically, after we assessed the selected supporting characteristics, we made an overall assessment for each of the five practices using the following scale:

- Followed or substantially followed—plans, policies, or processes have been developed and implemented properly for all or nearly all of the supporting characteristics.
- Partially followed—plans, policies, or processes have been developed and implemented properly for some of the supporting characteristics.
- Minimally or not followed—plans, policies, or processes are lacking for all or nearly all of the supporting characteristics.

To determine the extent to which the Federal Reserve followed these key practices and supporting characteristics, we reviewed agency documents and interviewed officials from the Federal Reserve and U.S. Mint. We also met with industry stakeholders (e.g., depository institution representatives and coin terminal operators) and academic and industry experts to discuss their views on the Federal Reserve's management of the circulating coin inventory and working relationships with other entities in the circulating coin supply chain.

To identify actions the Federal Reserve has taken to respond to potential changes in demand for coins and notes, we interviewed officials from the Federal Reserve, U.S. Mint, and Bureau of Engraving and Printing (BEP). We also interviewed depository institution representatives on the Customer Advisory Council, academic experts and industry representatives including coin terminal operators and Coinstar. We also interviewed government officials in Australia, Austria, and Canada to obtain their perspectives on potential changes in future cash demand. In addition, we reviewed Federal Reserve research and analysis pertaining to electronic and other payment methods including reports and documentation related to the CPO's long-term strategic framework and the Retail Payment's Office triennial payments studies from 2007 and 2010. We also interviewed Federal Reserve officials who have worked on these studies and obtained information about additional research efforts underway related to examining and preparing for changes in future demand for coins, notes, and other payment methods.

To identify actions taken by the Federal Reserve regarding the circulation of the $1 coin, we obtained perspectives on the availability and use of $1 coins from Federal Reserve and Reserve Bank officials. We also met with industry stakeholders and coin user groups—including depository institution representatives, the National Automated Merchandising Association, the Dollar Coin Alliance, Coinstar, and selected industry experts. We reviewed Federal Reserve and U.S. Mint responsibilities related to the circulation of the $1 coin, including those outlined in the Presidential $1 Coin Act of 2005 and Native American $1 Coin Act. To identify actions taken to identify, analyze, and overcome barriers to the circulation of the $1 coin, we reviewed the Federal Reserve's Annual Reports to Congress on the Presidential $1 Coin Program for 2007 through 2013 and interviewed Federal Reserve officials. In addition, we interviewed selected foreign government officials from Australia, Austria, and Canada to identify examples of actions taken to promote low denomination coins and to enhance the circulation of these coins in other countries. We also analyzed Federal Reserve data on $1 coin inventories, U.S. Mint orders, payments, and receipts from 2007 through 2012.

We assessed the reliability of data used in this chapter by (1) performing electronic testing of required data elements, (2) reviewing existing information about the data and the system that produced them, and (3) interviewing agency officials knowledgeable about the data. We determined that the data were sufficiently reliable for the purpose of this chapter.

We conducted this performance audit from March 2013 through October 2013 in accordance with generally accepted government auditing standards. Those standards require that we plan and perform the audit to obtain sufficient, appropriate evidence to provide a reasonable basis for our findings and conclusions based on our audit objectives. We believe that the evidence obtained provides a reasonable basis for our findings and conclusions based on our audit objectives.

APPENDIX II. DATA AND FIGURES ON COIN AND NOTE INVENTORY, ORDERS, AND CIRCULATION

Reserve Bank Coin Inventory and Inventory Targets

In 2009, the Federal Reserve's Cash Product Office (CPO) established national upper and lower inventory targets for pennies, nickels, dimes, and quarters to track and measure the coin inventory. National upper and lower inventory targets are reviewed and updated annually. In 2013, the upper national inventory targets were set based on the average peak Reserve Bank coin inventory from 2009 to 2012, and the lower national targets were set based on the 10 consecutive days from 2009 to 2012 with the most coin payments to depository institutions. Figures 9 through 12 present the Reserve Bank inventories of quarters, dimes, nickels and pennies from 2009 through 2012 and upper and lower national inventory targets from 2009 through 2013.[62]

Monthly Payments and Receipts for All Denominations

Coin receipts from depository institutions and Reserve Bank payments to depository institutions fluctuate throughout the year—reflecting changes in the public's spending patterns. (See Figure 13.) For example, in December 2012, the Federal Reserve paid about $479 million in coins to depository institutions (payments) and received about $452 million in coins from the depository institutions (receipts); this difference between payments and receipts is also referred to as net pay.

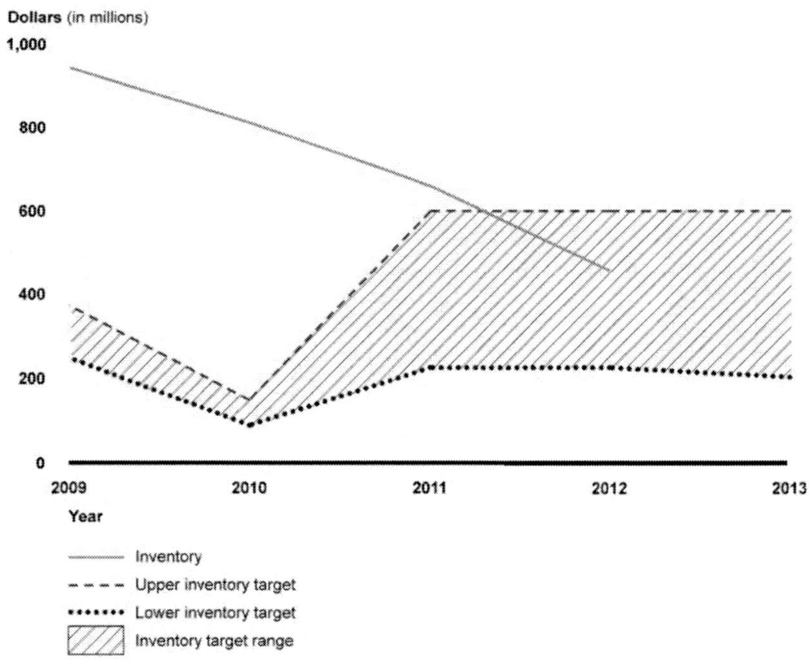

Source: GAO analysis of Federal Reserve data.

Figure 9. Reserve Bank Inventories of Quarters, 2009–2012, and National Inventory Targets, 2009–2013.

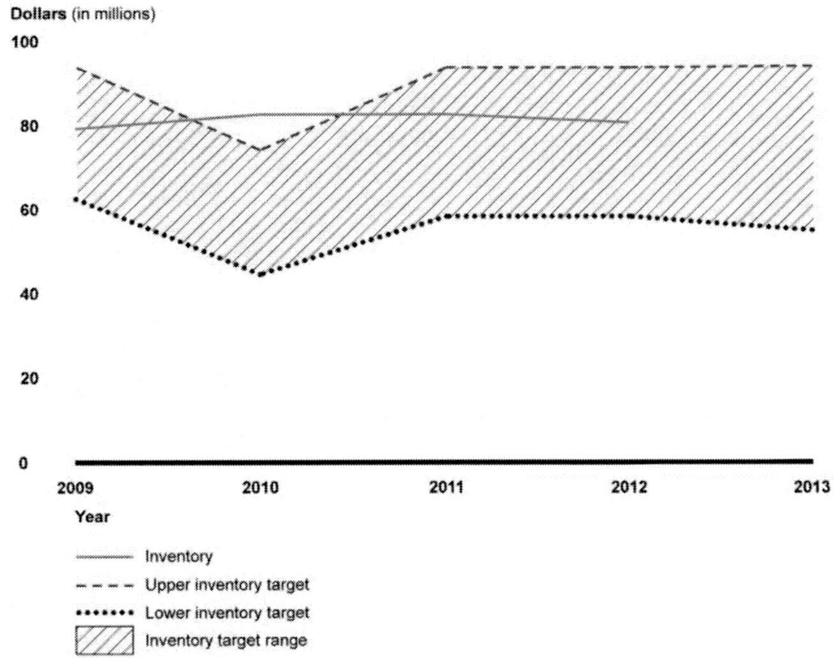

Source: GAO analysis of Federal Reserve data.

Figure 10. Reserve Bank Inventory of Dimes, 2009–2012, and National Inventory Targets, 2009–2013.

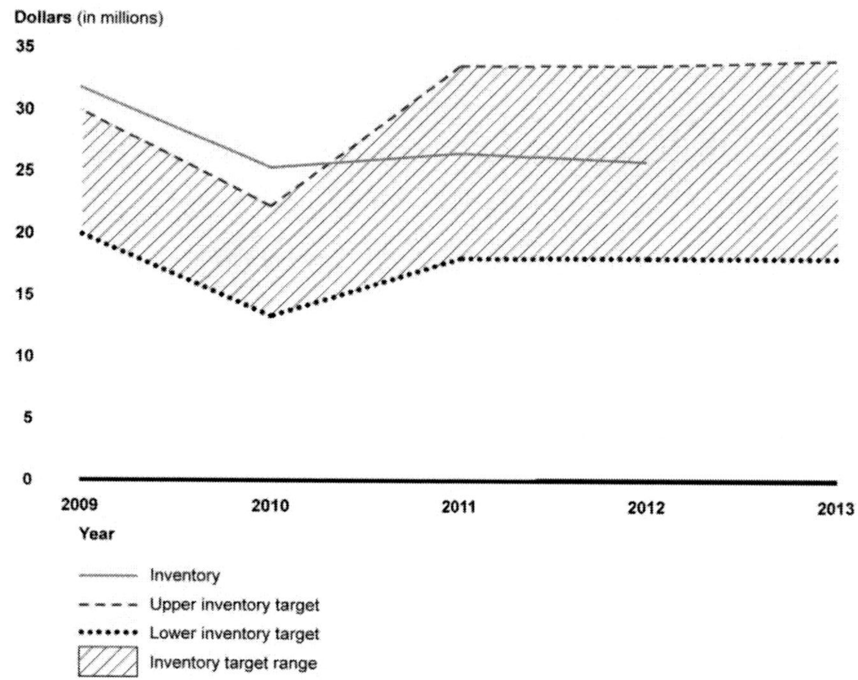

Source: GAO analysis of Federal Reserve data.

Figure 11. Reserve Bank Inventory of Nickels, 2009–2012, and National Inventory Targets, 2009–2013.

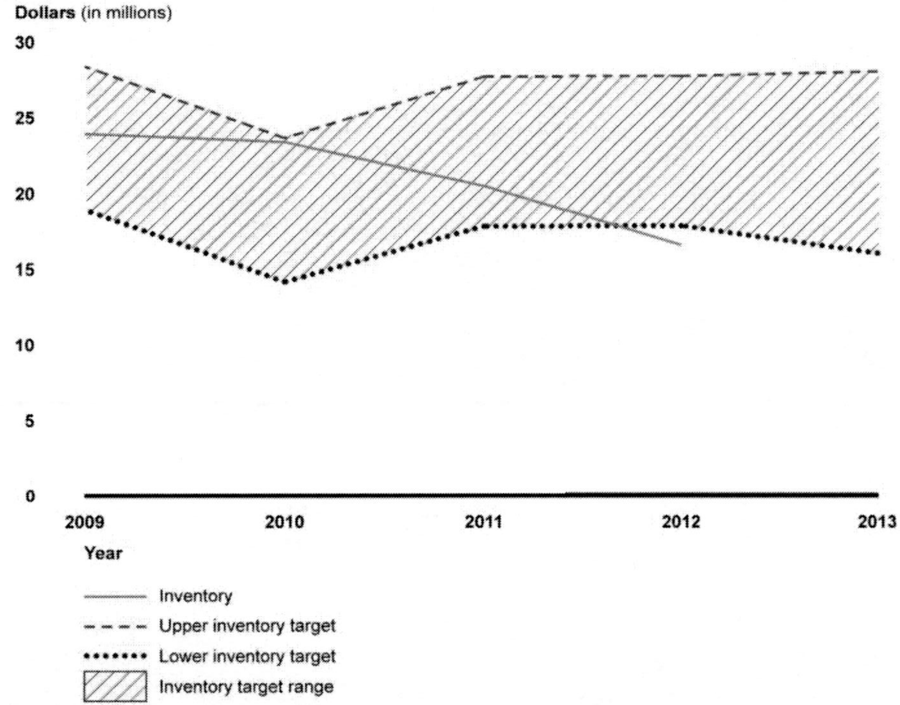

Source: GAO analysis of Federal Reserve data.

Figure 12. Reserve Bank Inventory of Pennies, 2009– 2012, and National Inventory Targets, 2009– 2013.

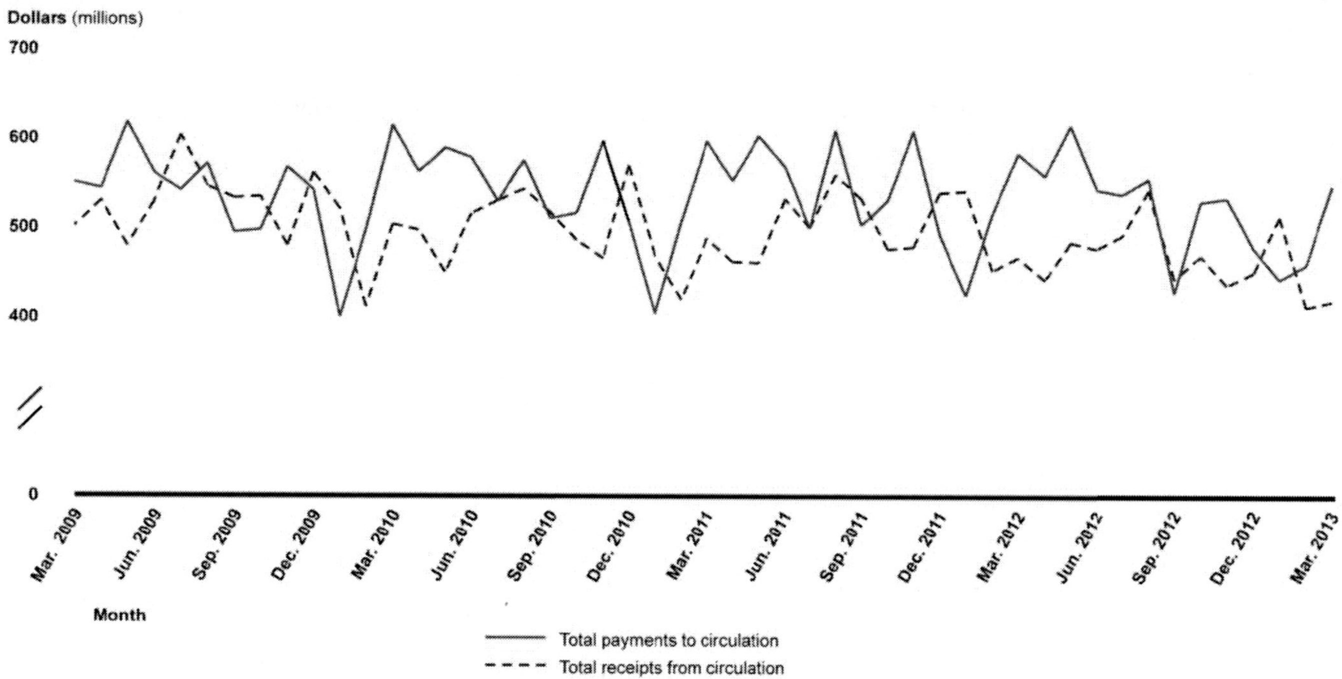

Source: GAO analysis of Federal Reserve data.

Figure 13. Monthly Reserve Bank Payments to and Receipts from Depository Institutions for All Denominations, March 2009– March 2013.

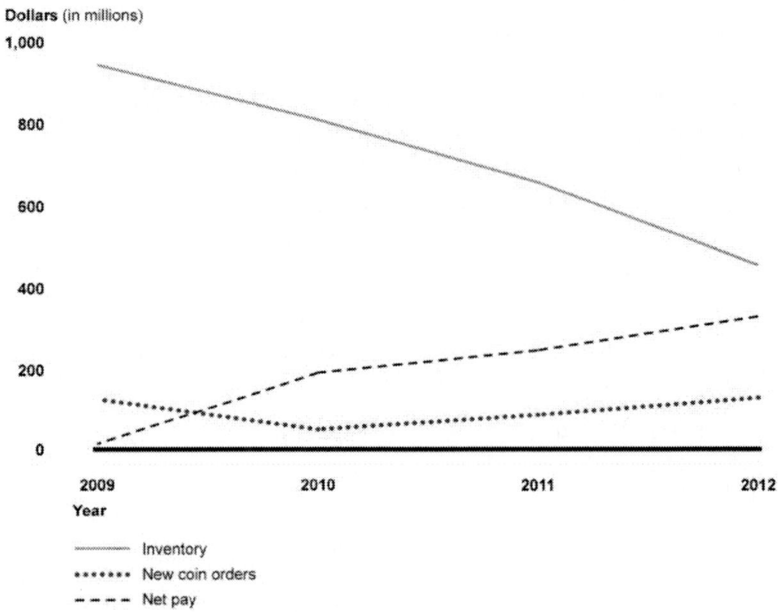

Source: GAO analysis of Federal Reserve data.

Figure 14. Reserve Bank Quarter Inventories, Net Pay, and New Coin Orders, 2009–2012.

Annual Net Pay, New Coin Orders, and Inventories for Quarters, Dimes, Nickels, and Pennies

Net pay is the difference between coins paid to depository institutions and coins received from depository institutions over a given period of time. Net pay greater than zero (positive) indicates that the Federal Reserve paid more coins to depository institutions than it received from depository institutions during that period (e.g., month or year). In addition, positive net pay indicates that additional coins—coins transferred from areas with negative net pay or new coins—are needed to meet demand. CPO uses national data on net pay, inventory, and expected changes to demand to make inventory management decisions such as where to transfer coin within and between Reserve Bank districts. When coin payments to depository institutions are greater than coin receipts from depository institutions, CPO orders new coins or uses circulated inventory to meet demand. Figures 14 through 17 present annual data for net pay, inventory, and new coin orders for quarters, dimes, nickels, and pennies from 2009 through 2012.[63]

Reserve Bank Costs Related to Coin

To manage the circulating coin inventory, Reserve Banks incur coin management costs and interbank transfer costs. The Reserve Banks' coin management costs include direct costs and support costs. (See Figure 18.) Direct costs are generally personnel costs such as salaries and benefits and support costs include utilities, protection, facilities, information technology, and other local and national support functions. From 2009 through 2012, direct costs represented about 30 percent and support costs represented about 70 percent of total coin management costs. Interbank transfers are shipments of coins from one Reserve Bank office region to another to ensure demand is met. (See Figure 19.)

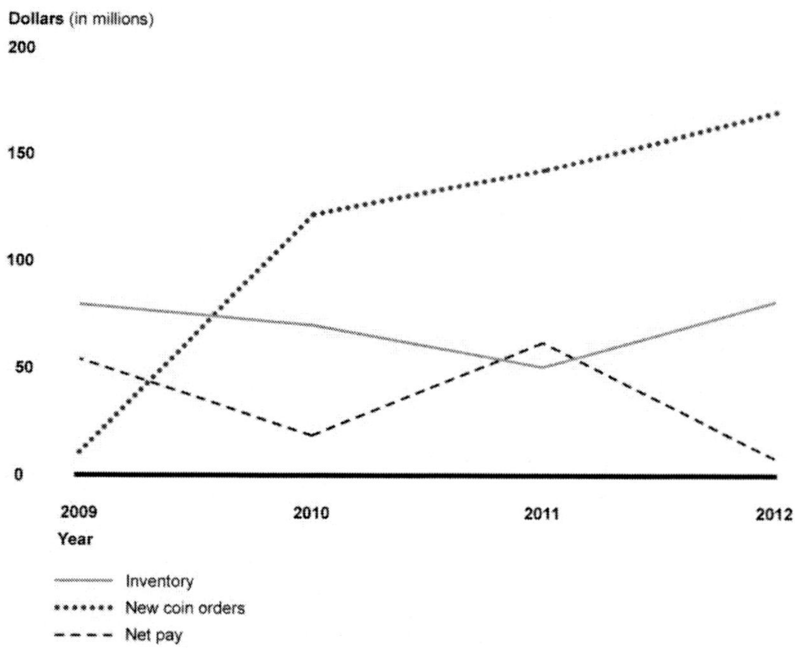

Source: GAO analysis of Federal Reserve data.

Figure 15. Reserve Bank Dime Inventories, Net Pay, and New Coin Orders, 2009–2012.

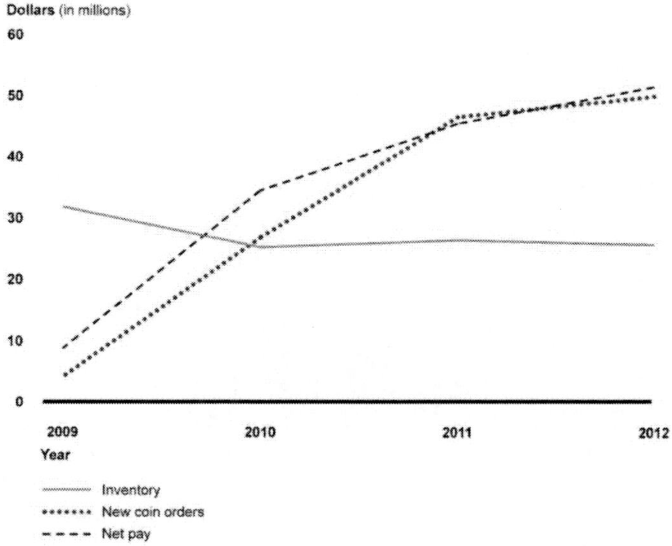

Source: GAO analysis of Federal Reserve data.

Figure 16. Reserve Bank Nickel Inventories, Net Pay, and New Coin Orders, 2009–2012.

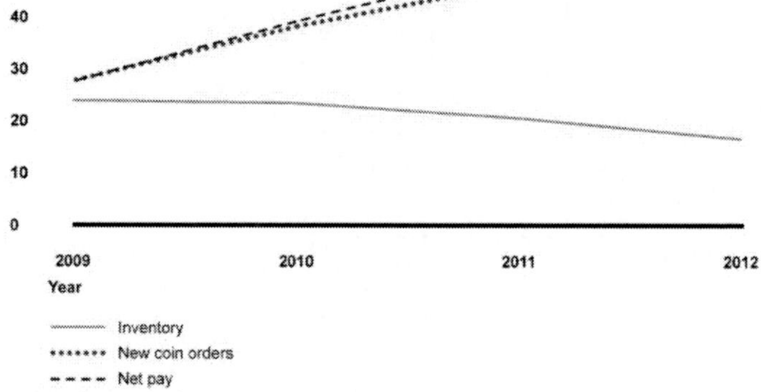

Source: GAO analysis of Federal Reserve data.

Figure 17. Reserve Bank Penny Inventories, Net Pay, and New Coin Orders, 2009–2012.

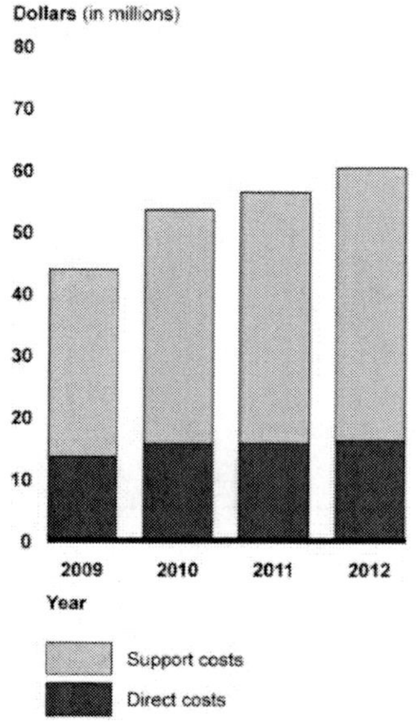

Source: GAO analysis of Federal Reserve data.

Figure 18. Total Reserve Bank Coin Management Costs, 2009–2012.

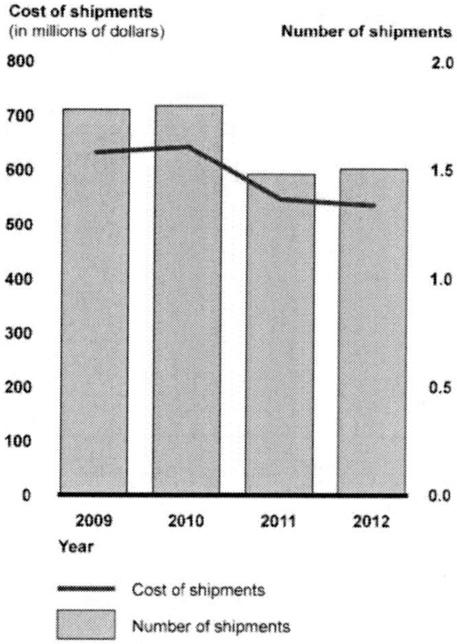

Source: GAO analysis of Federal Reserve data.

Figure 19. Number and Cost of Interbank Coin Shipments, 2009–2012.

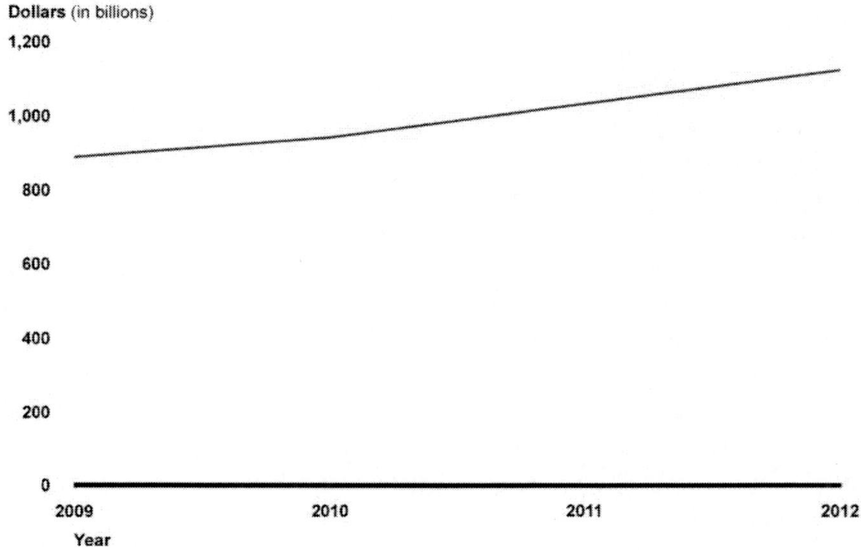

Source: GAO analysis of Treasury data.

Note: This represents the total face value of notes used as a medium of exchange that are in circulation. It includes some old and current notes that no longer circulate.

Figure 20. Value of Notes in Circulation, 2009–2012.

Notes in Circulation

From 2009 through 2012, the value of notes in circulation has increased by 27 percent from about $888 billion in 2009 to over $1,127 billion in 2012. (See Figure 20.)

Appendix III. Discussion of Key Practices for Managing the Coin Inventory

To effectively manage their inventory, private and governmental organizations involved in production and distribution operations use supply-chain and inventory-management practices. To assess the Federal Reserve's management of the circulating coin inventory we identified five key supply-chain management practices: collaboration, risk management, performance metrics, forecasting demand, and system optimization. Establishing, documenting, and following these practices and their supporting characteristics contributes to a more effective inventory management system. In addition, these supply-chain management practices are interrelated—as activities in one area may have implications in another—and can be used to achieve efficiency improvements and cost savings. For example, collaborative working relationships can improve risk management practices because information related to disruptions and actions to minimize or mitigate disruptions are more easily shared across the system.

To assess elements of the five key supply-chain management practices, we selected 14 supporting characteristics based on their relevance to coin inventory management. Based on our review, we determined whether the Federal Reserve's management of the circulating coin inventory followed or substantially followed, partially followed, or minimally or not followed each supporting characteristic. Our assessment of the characteristics served as the basis for our overall assessment as to whether each key practice was followed or substantially followed, partially followed, or minimally or not followed. For example, if we found supporting evidence that two of the three characteristics of a practice were substantially followed but no evidence to support that the third characteristic was followed we would determine that the key practice was partially followed.

Table 3. Collaboration and Supporting Characteristics

Key practice: Collaboration	**Overall assessment** ●
Collaboration is based on maintaining working relationships with partner entities across the supply chain by establishing policies, roles and responsibilities, and mechanisms for sharing information. Collaboration can be broadly defined as any joint activity that is intended to produce more public value than could be produced when the organizations act alone. GAO best practices for collaborative working relationships include, among other characteristics, agreeing on agency roles and responsibilities; establishing compatible policies, procedures, and other means to operate across agency boundaries; and developing mechanisms to monitor, evaluate and report results of collaborative efforts. In addition, according to APICS, building strategic partnerships is an effective way to reduce costs and improve service in the supply chain.	
Characteristics and coin inventory management examples	**Assessment of characteristics**
Characteristic: Develop and use policies or guidelines governing relationships with partner entities. *Example*: The Federal Reserve's Cash Product Office (CPO), on behalf of Reserve Banks, negotiated a contract with coin	●

Key practice: Collaboration	Overall assessment ●
terminal operators. The contract includes a coin terminal manual of operations, which standardized procedures and internal controls for the coin terminals' storage and handling of Reserve Bank coin across the 12 Reserve Bank districts.	
Characteristic: Agree upon roles and responsibilities with partner entities. *Example*: For interbank coin transfers, the U.S. Mint arranges transportation of coins across Reserve Banks; CPO reimburses the U.S. Mint for the costs of this transportation.	●
Characteristic: Develop and use mechanisms for sharing information related to the circulating coin inventory with partner entities. *Example*: FedLine, an online tool created for Reserve Bank customers (depository institutions) to access payment services, also provides a communication link between CPO, Reserve Bank offices, coin terminals, and depository institutions.	●

● Key practice followed or substantially followed—plans, policies, or processes have been developed and implemented properly for all or nearly all characteristics.

◐ Key practice partially followed—plans, policies, or processes have been developed and implemented properly for some characteristics.

○ Key practice minimally or not followed—plans, policies, or processes are lacking for all or nearly all characteristics.

Source: GAO analysis of Federal Reserve information.

Table 4. Risk Management and Supporting Characteristics

Key practice: Risk management	Overall assessment ●
Risk management is the planning and preparation for risks related to unanticipated events to help organizations respond to and maintain essential operations during events that could disrupt the normal flow of goods and materials within the supply chain. The Standard for Internal Control in the Federal Government and the Committee of Sponsoring Organizations of the Treadway Commission's (COSO) Internal Control—Integrated Framework require agencies to assess external and internal risks because conditions continually change, and to provide mechanisms to identify and deal with any special risks prompted by such changes. In addition, APICS recommends that supply chain management includes the management of risks surrounding unanticipated events that disrupt the normal flow of goods and materials within the supply chain.	

Table 4. (Continued)

Characteristics and coin inventory management examples	Assessment of characteristics
Characteristic: Identify sources of potential disruptions. *Example*: Federal Reserve officials identified disruptions that could affect regional coin supply chains (e.g., terrorist events, national weather disasters, or temporary events that limit transportation in metropolitan areas).	●
Characteristic: Assess the potential impact of the risk. *Example*: According to CPO officials, as soon as disruption is anticipated, they begin planning with stakeholders operating in the affected area, including Reserve Bank officials, coin terminal operators, and depository institutions. In addition, online resources are available for stakeholders to refer to.	●
Characteristic: Develop and use plans to mitigate the risk. *Example*: The 12 Reserve Banks have their own continuity of operations plans and each has a designated "buddy bank" to perform its functions, including coin circulation activities, in the event of a disruption. CPO will coordinate risk management efforts during a disruption for all Federal Reserve cash offices across the country.	●

● Key practice followed or substantially followed—plans, policies, or processes have been developed and implemented properly for all or nearly all characteristics.

◐ Key practice partially followed—plans, policies, or processes have been developed and implemented properly for some characteristics.

○ Key practice minimally or not followed—plans, policies, or processes are lacking for all or nearly all characteristics.

Source: GAO analysis of Federal Reserve information.

Table 5. Performance Metrics and Supporting Characteristics

Key practice: Performance metrics	Overall assessment ◐
Performance metrics involve the process of establishing, tracking, and reevaluating goals or metrics to measure change or improvement in a process or performance area. Performance goals and metrics should be clearly defined, measurable, actionable, relevant and timely, should be tracked to ensure that they are being met, and reevaluated periodically to ensure that they remain reasonable and useful. In addition, while it does not apply directly to the Federal Reserve, the GPRA Modernization Act of 2010 (GPRAMA) aims to ensure that federal agencies use performance information in decision making and holds them accountable for achieving results and improving government performance. We have previously	

Key practice: Performance metrics	Overall assessment ◐
reported that agencies should identify goals and establish a suite of performance metrics to determine whether they are meeting those goals.	
Characteristics and coin inventory management examples	**Assessment of characteristics**
Characteristic: Develop and use reasonable metrics that are clearly defined, measurable, actionable, relevant and timely. *Example*: In 2009, the Federal Reserve established upper and lower inventory targets for pennies, nickels, dimes, and quarters to track and measure the national coin inventory and inventory at each Reserve Bank office and coin terminal. However, CPO does not have additional goals and metrics to measure other aspects of its management of the coin inventory.	◐
Characteristic: Track progress against metrics or targets. *Example*: CPO tracks national and local inventory levels to ensure that the national coin supply and local inventories are within inventory targets.	●
Characteristic: Establish a process to reevaluate metrics or targets. *Example*: CPO reevaluates the national inventory targets annually; however, it has not established a process for reevaluating its methodology for setting local inventory levels.	◐

● Key practice followed or substantially followed—plans, policies, or processes have been developed and implemented properly for all or nearly all characteristics.

◐ Key practice partially followed—plans, policies, or processes have been developed and implemented properly for some characteristics.

○ Key practice minimally or not followed—plans, policies, or processes are lacking for all or nearly all characteristics.

Source: GAO analysis of Federal Reserve information.

Table 6. Forecasting Demand and Supporting Characteristics

Key practice: Forecasting demand	Overall assessment ◐
Planning and forecasting for demand involves preparing for and estimating expected changes in future demand and planning and making decisions based on these estimates. Forecasts are developed in order to better estimate future demand and planning decisions are based on these forecasts to meet the expected changes in demand. According to APICS, forecasting is attempting to predict or project future statistics—typically, demand or sales. It requires that	

Table 6. (Continued)

Key practice: Forecasting demand	Overall assessment ◐
all factors surrounding the decision-making process are recorded. Factors that affect forecasting include sales demand patterns, economic conditions, competitor actions, market research, product mixes, and pricing and promotional activities. Forecasts can be made at strategic, tactical, and operational levels. The forecasting process predicts demand and the use of products and services so that the right quantities are ordered in advance. In forecasting, either historical demand data are transformed into future projections or a subjective prediction of the future is made—or some combination of the two.	
Characteristics and coin inventory management examples	**Assessment of characteristics**
Characteristic: Have a process in place to forecast demand. *Example*: Since 2009, the Federal Reserve has used a proprietary inventory management system to track circulating coin inventory and forecast future needs.	●
Characteristic: Use forecast results to plan and manage the circulating coin inventory. *Example*: Information from the proprietary system is used to develop forecasts of expected coin payments, receipts, and inventory for each distribution location and this information is used to determine if new coins should be ordered from the U.S. Mint or shipped from one location to another.	●
Characteristic: Assess forecast accuracy. *Example*: CPO lacks a method to assess or track forecast accuracy related to monthly coin orders. According to CPO officials, they compare the U.S. Mint's actual coin shipment to their initial coin order by reviewing annual data, but they have not established or tracked any performance measures related to the accuracy of their monthly forecast.	○

● Key practice followed or substantially followed—plans, policies, or processes have been developed and implemented properly for all or nearly all characteristics.

◐ Key practice partially followed—plans, policies, or processes have been developed and implemented properly for some characteristics.

○ Key practice minimally or not followed—plans, policies, or processes are lacking for all or nearly all characteristics.

Source: GAO analysis of Federal Reserve information.

Table 7. System Optimization and Supporting Characteristics

Key practice: System optimization	Overall assessment ◐
System optimization involves considering, as a whole, the strategic interactions and operations of the entire supply chain or inventory process in developing process change. According to APICS, optimizing the logistics network is the process of achieving the most efficient network to move materials and products from the supplier through the manufacturing process to the end user. For example, to improve its inventory management, the Department of Defense has taken steps to collect information from all tiers of its supply chain and use that information to make decisions on movements of inventory and has developed models to inform them of the optimal use of its inventories.	
Characteristics and coin inventory management examples	**Assessment of characteristics**
Characteristic: Obtain access to information and resources from across the circulating coin supply chain (e.g., knowledge of coin production lead-time, inventory, demand and transportation). *Example*: CPO has multiple systems that provide information from across the supply chain and help make decisions based on current and expected changes to demand and inventory. This information includes coin management costs and actual and forecasted coin demand. Regular communications with key supply-chain stakeholder representatives from Reserve Banks, depository institutions, coin terminals, and the U.S. Mint provide CPO with information such as market changes that could influence changes in demand and challenges that could limit the efficient distribution of coins.	●
Characteristic: Use information and resources to identify and implement efficiencies within the supply chain. *Example*: CPO's use of information and resources is limited thereby making it difficult to track progress for continued improvement or understand the extent to which these strategic interactions optimize the overall efficiency of its management of the circulating coin inventory. For example, the U.S. Mint's production of new coin could be more efficient with improvements to the accuracy of new coin orders. Currently, the U.S. Mint produces a safety stock, in part, to ensure it is able to produce enough coins to fulfill CPO's final, adjusted order. Therefore, more accurate forecasts and coin orders could lessen the need for the U.S. Mint to produce safety stock. Key supply chain stakeholders can also act as a resource for the CPO to identify efficiencies within the supply chain.	○

● Key practice followed or substantially followed—plans, policies, or processes have been developed and implemented properly for all or nearly all characteristics.

◐ Key practice partially followed—plans, policies, or processes have been developed and implemented properly for some characteristics.
○ Key practice minimally or not followed—plans, policies, or processes are lacking for all or nearly all characteristics.
Source: GAO analysis of Federal Reserve information.

End Notes

[1] The total amount of coins in circulation is comprised of coins held by the Reserve Banks and coins in general circulation (e.g., coins held by businesses or the public).

[2] For the purposes of this chapter, the term "Federal Reserve" refers to the Board of Governors of the Federal Reserve System as well as the Reserve Banks.

[3] Committee of Sponsoring Organizations of the Treadway Commission, *Internal Control—Integrated Framework* (1992). COSO is a joint initiative of five professional associations dedicated to providing thought leadership through the development of frameworks and guidance on enterprise risk management, internal control, and fraud deterrence.

[4] While there are many other leading supply-chain management practices and supporting characteristics, we selected and validated a sample of those most relevant to our review. In addition, academic and industry experts in operations and supply chain management validated that the selected key practices, definitions, and supporting characteristics were relevant to coin inventory management.

[5] We reviewed supply-chain-management and operations-management leading practices, our past defense inventory management and Government Performance and Results Act reports, and academic literature to identify those practices applicable to the circulating coin inventory. Selected experts and foreign government officials reviewed and validated that the five key practices identified were relevant to coin inventory management.

[6] Funds derived from assessments imposed by the Board are not to be considered governmental funds or appropriated monies. 12 U.S.C. § 244.

[7] The General Fund refers to Treasury accounts that hold federal receipts not allocated by law for a specific purpose and includes money collected from taxes, customs duties, and revenues generated by government agencies.

[8] The revolving fund of the U.S. Mint is financed through the U.S. Mint Public Enterprise Fund. The difference between the face value of minted circulating coins and the cost of their production, including the cost of metal used in the minting and the cost of transporting the coins to Reserve Banks for distribution to the public is referred to as "seigniorage."

[9] In its 2012 Annual Report, the U.S. Mint reported an on-budget transfer of $77 million to the General Fund for fiscal year 2012. However, the U.S. Mint did not make off-budget transfers to the General Fund in 2012 because it determined that amounts resulting from the sale of circulating coins were required to mitigate the risks of future economic uncertainty, impacts from continued penny and nickel losses, and loss of revenue from the suspension of $1 coin production.

[10] GAO, *U.S. Coins: The Federal Reserve Banks Are Fulfilling Coin Demand, but Optimal Inventory Ranges Are Undefined*, GAO-08-401 (Washington, D.C.: Mar. 21, 2008).

[11] Circulating coins are available to the public (e.g., for general use in commerce), and are distinguished from coins produced and sold as collectibles.

[12] 12 U.S.C. §§ 411 and 414.

[13] S. 1105, the Currency Optimization, Innovation, and National Savings Act.

[14] GAO, *U.S. Coins: Benefits and Considerations for Replacing the $1 Note with a $1 Coin*, GAO-13-164T (Washington, D.C.: Nov. 29, 2012). GAO-13-164T assumed a lower

replacement ratio than past GAO reports assessing the impacts of replacing the $1 note. In addition, the life of the note has increased with new processing equipment.

[15] In commenting on this chapter, Federal Reserve officials noted that previous GAO analyses and the associated potential savings were due to increased seigniorage income and not to production costs savings. Additionally, they noted that other societal costs and benefits—such as costs related to transitioning to $1 coins—were not included in GAO's analysis.

[16] Pub. L. No. 109-145, § 104, 119 Stat. 2664, 2670 (2005), codified at 31 U.S.C. § 5112(p).

[17] GAO, *U.S. Coins: Replacing the $1 Note with a $1 Coin Would Provide a Financial Benefit to the Government*, GAO-11-281 (Washington, D.C.: Mar. 4, 2011).

[18] For more information on earlier Reserve Bank coin management practices see GAO-08-401.

[19] From 2004 to 2008, Reserve Bank combined inventory for pennies, nickels, dimes, and quarters was on average about $700 million per year. Information on the inventory of $1 coins is presented later in this chapter.

[20] The upper national inventory targets for 2013 are set based on the average peak Reserve Bank coin inventory from 2009 to 2010, and the lower national targets are set based on the 10 consecutive days from 2009 to 2012 when the most coin was paid to depository institutions. According to CPO officials, the lower target protects against the Federal Reserve's running out of coin during an extended period of time without deposits (10 days) and temporary dips below the lower target should not be construed as not having enough coins to meet demand during normal conditions.

[21] CPO officials attributed exceeding upper inventory targets for quarters to the end of the 50 State Quarter Program, which increased Reserve Bank inventory of quarters, and to lower demand for quarters during the financial crisis.

[22] CPO told us that in 2012 Reserve Banks had a sufficient supply of pennies to meet demand and attributed not meeting the lower targets to fluctuations in the payments and receipts of pennies. The lower inventory target for pennies was decreased by approximately 10 percent from 2012 to 2013.

[23] A "payable day" is the amount of coin inventory needed to meet one day of expected payments to depository institutions. Some Reserve Bank offices provide long-term storage of excess inventory of quarters, half dollars, and $1 coins in addition to storing transactional levels of all denominations to support local demand.

[24] In 1999 and 2000 shortages for quarters and pennies in certain parts of the country were reported.

[25] Between 2009 and 2012, the average cost of an interbank transfer was around $2,200. Our analysis of CPO and U.S. Mint data indicated that there were more interbank transfers in 2009 and 2010 than in 2011 and 2012. See figure 19 in appendix II.

[26] On a monthly basis, the U.S. Mint produces safety stock equivalent to the average deviation between past CPO initial orders and actual shipments. In addition to helping the U.S. Mint respond to changes in monthly coin orders, producing safety stock also helps the U.S. Mint respond to seasonal changes in coin demand.

[27] Between 2004 and 2007, more than $900 million worth of new pennies, nickels, dimes, and quarters were ordered each year. Information on orders of $1 coins is presented later in this chapter.

[28] These costs are indirect costs to the government because the Federal Reserve and U.S. Mint incur the costs and the amounts they remit to the U.S. Treasury are less the costs related to coins.

[29] In 2012 there were about 600 interbank transfers costing about $1.3 million. For more information on interbank transfer expenses see figure 19 in appendix II.

[30] Since 2006, the costs of producing pennies and nickels have been above the face value of these coins. For example, in fiscal year 2012, the penny cost the U.S. Mint 2 cents to produce. This represents negative seigniorage because the face value was less than the cost of production for these denominations.

[31] Federal Reserve, *Strategic Framework 2012-15* (2013).

[32] Committee of Sponsoring Organizations of the Treadway Commission, *Internal Control—Integrated Framework* (1992).

[33] Each Reserve Bank independently manages and is responsible for establishing and maintaining internal controls over its financial reporting and recording. The Federal Reserve's cost accounting system allocates costs based on the percentage of time employees spend on an activity, and Reserve Banks may vary in their assignment of activity costs across locations within their districts. In addition, personnel allocate their time across activities such as note processing and destruction or coin paying, receiving, and verification, rather than directly charging specific time to a function such as coin management. According to CPO officials, the amount of time spent on an activity is determined through an annual employee survey that tracks the time employees spend on various activities.

[34] In 2012, costs related to coins represented 11 percent of overall currency management costs, and currency management costs represented approximately 21 percent of Reserve Bank costs. From 2008 to 2012, Reserve Bank currency management direct costs increased by 10 percent and support costs increased 30 percent. In addition, from 2008 through 2012, according to the Federal Reserve's Annual Budget Reviews, overall Reserve Bank operation costs increased by 49 percent from $1.7 billion to $2.5 billion.

[35] Between 2008 and 2012, similar to currency management costs, direct costs represented about 30 percent of coin management costs and support costs represented the remaining 70 percent.

[36] From 2008 through 2012, across the 28 Reserve Bank locations personnel costs increased from about $9 million to about $13 million and the average number of personnel increased from about 110 to 135.

[37] Costs related to centralized coin management—such as CPO operations—are distributed across the individual Reserve Banks.

[38] Federal Reserve coins are transported and distributed in standard-sized bags. These standard bags of loose coins (new and circulated coins) contain $50 in pennies, $200 in nickels, $1,000 in dimes, $1,000 in quarters, $1,000 in half dollars, and $2,000 in $1 coins.

[39] According to CPO officials, two of the 28 Federal Reserve offices fully outsource coin services to coin terminals in their markets, and the other 26 Reserve Bank offices provide coin services on-site.

[40] For additional information on these key practices and supporting characteristics as well as our analysis for each supporting characteristic, see appendix III.

[41] The difference between payments to and receipts from depository institutions is referred to as "net pay" and is used by CPO to help determine general coin demand nationwide and at individual locations.

[42] GPRA sought to focus federal agencies on performance by requiring agencies to develop long-term and annual goals—contained in strategic and annual performance plans—and measure and report on progress towards those goals on an annual basis (Pub. L. No. 103-62, 107 Stat. 285 (Aug. 3, 1993)). The GPRA Modernization Act of 2010 (GPRAMA) enhances GPRA and provides important tools that can help inform congressional and executive branch decision making to address challenges the federal government faces (Pub. L. No. 111-352, 124 Stat. 3866 (Jan. 4, 2011)). Among other things, GPRAMA requires that agencies establish priority goals and metrics and report on them quarterly. These goals include performance and efficiency improvements to program activities, regulations, policies, and agency management.

[43] GAO, *Managing for Results: Executive Branch Should More Fully Implement the GPRA Modernization Act to Address Pressing Governance Challenges,* GAO-13-518 (Washington, D.C.: June 26, 2013).

[44] GAO, *Managing for Results: Enhancing Agency Use of Performance Information for Management Decision Making,* GAO-05-927 *(Washington, D.C.: Sep. 9, 2005) and GAO, Managing for Results: A Guide for Using the GPRA Modernization Act to Help Inform Congressional Decision Making,* GAO-12-621SP (Washington, D.C.: June 15, 2012).

[45] In addition to producing and issuing coins, the Australian, Austrian, and Canadian mints are responsible for distributing coin and managing their circulating coin inventories.

[46] Various methods can be used to assess forecast accuracy. Examples of methods commonly used in operations management include mean absolute deviation, absolute percent of error, and tracking signal. Tracking signal can be used to assess bias in a forecast by measuring the variation between the forecast and demand for several consecutive periods.

[47] According to CPO officials, demand for coin fluctuates throughout the year based on seasonal changes in public demand and receipts from depository institutions and these fluctuations in coin demand can be volatile. For more information on seasonal fluctuations in coin demand see Figure 13 in appendix II.

[48] APICS, *Principles of Operations Planning: Demand Management* (Chicago, IL: 2013).

[49] Logistics Management Institute, *Lifecycle Forecasting Improvement: Causative Research and Item Introduction Phase,* Report DL920T1 (November 2010).

[50] Producing "safety stock" also helps the U.S. Mint respond to seasonal changes in coin demand. The U.S. Mint can smooth production throughout the year rather than ramp production up or down in response to seasonal increases or decreases in demand. Regarding the use of safety stock for meeting adjustments in monthly orders, according to U.S. Mint officials, the costs related to storing this stock are less than the alternative of hiring additional staff or paying overtime to produce more coins if additional production was required to meet the final order. Thus, the benefit of holding safety stock relates both to promoting level-loading production over the course of time as well as helping to ensure that adequate stock is on hand even if final coin orders exceed initial forecasted orders.

[51] Traditionally, as the economy and population grow, the demand for currency also grows. However, it is difficult to know whether this relationship might change in the future if, as expected, financial transactions become increasingly conducted electronically.

[52] Federal Reserve System, *The 2010 Federal Reserve Payments Study* (2011). This study includes the most recently available data on payment trends. The 2013 study will present similar data for 2009–2012 and is expected to be complete later this year.

[53] Due to the December 2011 Treasury decision to cease production of new $1 coins for circulation, the Federal Reserve's current management of the $1 coin inventory is focused on managing those $1 coins already in storage or circulation.

[54] 12 U.S.C. § 418.

[55] Although production of circulating Presidential $1 Coins was suspended in 2011, collectible versions continue to be available through the U.S. Mint's website. The public and collectors are able to directly order Presidential $1 coin rolls, bags, and boxes.

[56] The U.S. Mint has issued $1 coins featuring Presidents in sequential order and every Reserve Bank office has had unmixed supplies of the coins available for a 6-week special ordering period to allow members of the public to order coins featuring a specific President.

[57] 31 U.S.C. §5112(p).

[58] 31 USC 5112(p)(3)(B).

[59] GAO-11-281.

[60] Committee of Sponsoring Organizations of the Treadway Commission, *Internal Control—Integrated Framework* (1992).

[61] For example, GAO, *Defense Inventory: Actions Underway to Implement Improvement Plan but Steps Needed to Enhance Efforts,* GAO-12-493 *(Washington, D.C.: May 3, 2012) and Managing for Results: Executive Branch Should More Fully Implement the GPRA Modernization Act to Address Pressing Governance Challenges*, GAO-13-518 (Washington, D.C.: June 26, 2013).

[62] 2012 annual Reserve Bank inventory data on quarters, dimes, nickels and pennies and 2013 national upper and lower inventory targets was the most recent available.

[63] These figures do not include coin payments made directly to circulation by the U.S. Mint. Information on net pay, coin orders, and inventory of $1 coins is presented in the body of this chapter.

In: U.S. Circulating Coins
Editor: Catherine Solorio

ISBN: 978-1-63117-184-0

Chapter 2

U.S. COINS: THE FEDERAL RESERVE BANKS ARE FULFILLING COIN DEMAND, BUT OPTIMAL INVENTORY RANGES ARE UNDEFINED*

United States Government Accountability Office

WHY GAO DID THIS STUDY

Federal Reserve Banks fulfill the coin demand of the nation's depository institutions—which include commercial banks, savings and loan associations, and credit unions—by ordering new coins from the U.S. Mint and managing coins held in inventory at the Reserve Banks and in coin terminals. Reliably estimating the demand for coins and efficiently managing the inventory of circulated coins is important to ensure that depository institutions have enough coins to meet the public's demand and to avoid unnecessary coin production costs. Since late 2006, rising metal prices have driven the costs of producing pennies and nickels above the face values of the coins. This chapter addresses (1) the Reserve Banks' process for ordering and distributing coins to the nation's depository institutions and (2) the extent to which this process meets depository institutions' demand for coins.

---

* This is an edited, reformatted and augmented version of a United States Government Accountability Office Publication, GAO-08-401, dated March, 2008.

GAO interviewed officials responsible for coin distribution at each of the 12 Reserve Banks and met with representatives of 4 large operators of Federal Reserve coin terminals, 2 banking associations, the U.S. Mint, and the nation's largest coin recycling company. GAO also analyzed Reserve Bank data for fiscal years 1993 through 2007.

Federal Reserve and U.S. Mint officials generally agreed with GAO's findings in the chapter and provided technical comments, which were incorporated as appropriate.

WHAT GAO FOUND

The Reserve Banks' process for ordering and distributing coins uses new coins ordered from the U.S. Mint, circulated coins in inventory, and transfers of circulated coins to meet depository institutions' demand for coins. New coin orders begin each month with a recommendation generated by a forecasting tool. Each Reserve Bank office then refines this recommendation in light of its current inventory holdings and its knowledge of local factors that may affect demand, such as changes in a transit authority's use of coins. Each office next submits a request for coins to the Reserve Banks' national Cash Product Office (CPO). CPO seeks to fill the request with transfers of circulated coins from other offices before it consolidates the requests and submits a monthly order for new coins to the U.S. Mint. In fiscal years 2006 and 2007, CPO used transfers to reduce its new coin orders by approximately 10 percent.

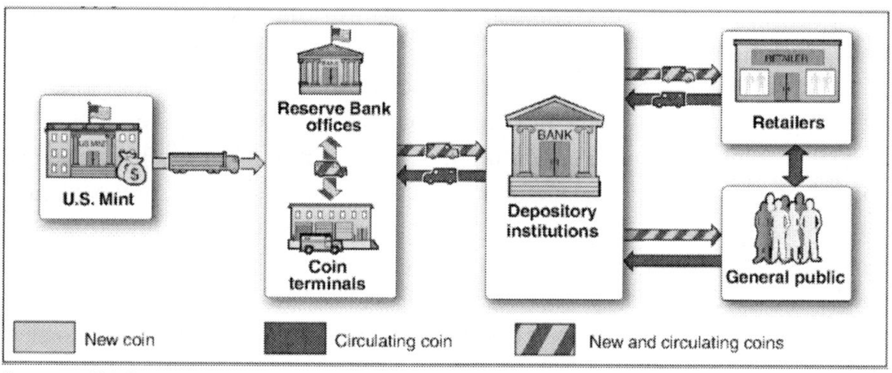

Source: GAO.

Coin Supply and Distribution Process.

The Reserve Banks' process for ordering and distributing coins has met depository institutions' demand since fiscal year 2000, but the process does not define optimal coin inventory ranges. Currently, each Reserve Bank office sets and manages its own inventory levels, resulting in varying levels of inventory held relative to demand. Overall, inventory levels for most denominations have generally been decreasing since fiscal year 2001, yet inventory levels are more likely to be high than low relative to demand, because, for the Reserve Banks, the risk of not meeting depository institutions' demand for coins far exceeds the risk of holding too many coins in inventory. However, holding coins in inventory that could be used to fulfill demand elsewhere can be inefficient, resulting in new coin production costs that could have been avoided if coins held in inventory had been used instead. To increase the efficiency of the Reserve Banks' process, CPO plans this year to begin implementing a new approach to inventory management that it piloted in 2006 and found effective. Under this approach, CPO will determine the number of circulated and new coins each district will receive monthly and will be responsible for ensuring that the Reserve Bank offices maintain appropriate inventory levels.

March 21, 2008

The Honorable Luis V. Gutierrez
Chairman
The Honorable Ron Paul
Ranking Member
Subcommittee on Domestic and International Monetary Policy,
Trade, and Technology
Committee on Financial Services
House of Representatives

The Federal Reserve Banks (Reserve Banks) and the U.S. Mint both play a role in ensuring that the economy has an adequate supply of coins for trade and commerce. The Reserve Banks fulfill the coin demand of the nation's depository institutions—which include commercial banks, savings and loan associations, and credit unions—by ordering new coins from the U.S. Mint and managing an inventory of circulated coins stored in Reserve Banks and coin terminals throughout the nation. In 2007, the U.S. Mint produced 15.4 billion coins, with a value of about $2 billion. According to the Department of the Treasury, as of November 30, 2007, coins worth approximately $37 billion were in circulation throughout the country. Reliably estimating the demand for new coins and efficiently managing the inventory of circulated coins is important—first, to ensure that the depository institutions have enough coins to meet the public's demand and, second, to avoid unnecessary coin production costs. During the fourth quarter of 2006, rising metal prices drove the costs of producing pennies and nickels above the face values of these coins.[1] According to the U.S. Mint's 2007 annual report, the penny costs 1.7 cents to produce and the nickel costs 9.5 cents.[2]

The Federal Reserve System is composed of a central, governmental agency—the Board of Governors (Board)—and 12 regional Reserve Banks, each of which is located in a Federal Reserve district. The Reserve Banks are the operating arms of the central banking system. They carry out a variety of Federal Reserve System functions, including operating a nationwide payment system and distributing the nation's currency and coin. The Reserve Banks have 30 offices that, among other responsibilities, provide coins to depository institutions. The Reserve Banks' national Cash Product Office (CPO), located at the Federal Reserve Bank of San Francisco, coordinates coin distribution from a national perspective as one of its responsibilities. The Reserve Banks store coins on-site and at about 180 coin terminals located throughout the country. The coin terminals provide additional storage space for coins and help to facilitate their distribution. You asked us to examine the processes for ordering and distributing all denominations of coins without creating excess inventory. Accordingly, this chapter addresses (1) the Reserve Banks' process for ordering and distributing coins and (2) the extent to which this process meets the depository institutions' demand for coins.[3]

To determine the Reserve Banks' process for ordering and distributing coins, we reviewed relevant reports and research papers on how the Reserve Banks and the U.S. Mint determine the number of coins to be produced and distributed. We interviewed Federal Reserve economists and Board and Reserve Bank officials representing the 30 Reserve Bank offices to understand how the Reserve Bank offices develop orders for new coins from the U.S. Mint and manage their coin inventory levels. We also interviewed key stakeholders—including officials from the U.S. Mint, operators of coin terminals with agreements to store Reserve Bank coin inventory, and representatives of banking associations—to determine how the Reserve Banks work in collaboration with others to identify and fulfill the depository institutions' requests for coins. We analyzed information on the costs paid by the U.S. Mint to transport circulated coins and analyzed the number of transfers between Reserve Banks from fiscal years 2002 through 2007.

To determine the extent to which the Reserve Banks' process meets the demand for coins, we obtained data on the Reserve Banks' coin payments to depository institutions, receipts for coins deposited by the depository institutions, orders for new coins, and inventory levels for fiscal years 1993 through 2007 for each coin denomination and Reserve Bank.[4] We analyzed these data to identify the demand for coins, the extent to which the Reserve Banks order new coins to meet demand, and the amount of inventory available to meet demand. We presented our data on a fiscal year (October through September) basis because the U.S. Mint operates on a fiscal year; however, the Reserve Banks operate on a calendar year. To assess the reliability of the Reserve Banks' coin data, we talked with agency officials about data quality control procedures and reviewed relevant documentation. We determined that these data were sufficiently reliable for the purposes of this chapter. We interviewed Reserve Bank officials to discuss factors affecting trends in the data and the Reserve Banks' approach to coin inventory management. We also interviewed two banking associations and the four coin terminal operators with the most agreements to store Reserve Bank coin inventory to obtain their views on the Reserve Banks' process for fulfilling depository institutions' demand for coins. We conducted this performance audit from April 2007 through March 2008 in accordance with generally accepted government auditing standards. Those standards require that we plan and perform the audit to obtain sufficient, appropriate evidence to provide a reasonable basis for our findings and conclusions based on our audit objectives. We believe that the evidence obtained provides a reasonable basis for our findings and conclusions based on our audit objectives. More details about our objectives, scope, and methodology appear in appendix I.

RESULTS IN BRIEF

The Reserve Banks' process for ordering and distributing coins uses new coins ordered from the U.S. Mint, circulated coins held in inventory, and transfers of circulated coins between Reserve Bank offices to meet the depository institutions' demand. To develop orders for new coins, the Reserve Bank offices combine coin demand forecasts, local information, and CPO's assessment of opportunities to redistribute circulated coins between Reserve Bank offices. Every month, the Reserve Bank offices receive recommended coin orders generated by a forecasting tool that is maintained by the Economic Research Group at the Federal Reserve Bank of San Francisco. Each office then compares its current inventory levels with the inventory levels it wants to hold to meet demand and considers factors that may affect demand within its jurisdiction to refine the recommended coin order. Such factors may include coin recycling activity (i.e., the extent to which the public uses coin-counting machines, such as Coinstar, to trade in coins for currency or some form of credit, such as a gift card); the issuance of a commemorative circulating coin; and transit authorities' or casinos' use of coins. Once a Reserve Bank office has considered these factors, it adjusts the tool's recommended coin order and then sends a request for coins to CPO. CPO reviews the offices' requests for coins from a national perspective and looks for opportunities to fill those requests by transferring circulated coins between Reserve Bank offices, rather than ordering new coins. Reserve Bank data show that CPO reduced orders for new coins by approximately 10 percent in fiscal years 2006 and 2007 by fulfilling the Reserve Bank offices' requests with transfers of circulated coins from other offices. Once CPO has identified circulated coins that can be transferred to fulfill the Reserve Bank offices' requests for coins, CPO reduces the offices' orders for new coins, consolidates all of the orders, and sends the final order to the U.S. Mint.

The Reserve Banks' process for distributing coins has met depository institutions' demand since fiscal year 2000, but the process does not define optimal coin inventory ranges for Reserve Bank offices to hold to meet demand. Our analysis of the Reserve Banks' coin order, inventory, payment, and receipt data showed that the Reserve Banks maintained enough inventory to meet demand, even when demand was greater than anticipated. In addition, our analysis showed that overall inventory levels for most denominations have generally been decreasing since fiscal year 2001. However, the Reserve Banks have taken a decentralized approach to inventory management that allows the Reserve Bank offices to determine what inventory levels they should keep on hand to meet future demand and avoid the risk of shortages. Specifically, each Reserve Bank office sets and manages its own inventory levels, resulting in varying levels of inventory being held by the Reserve Banks relative to demand. Reserve Bank officials expressed no concern about holding too many coins and told us that excess inventory is an issue only when coin inventories approach storage capacity limits. However, with rare exceptions, the Reserve Banks have more storage capacity than they need to maintain their current inventory levels; therefore, storage capacity limits do not create an incentive to determine and manage to optimal coin inventory ranges. CPO and Reserve Bank officials noted that the risk of not meeting depository institutions' demand for coins far exceeds the risk of having too many coins in inventory, and that it is easier to deplete coin inventories than to build them up. However, holding coins in inventory that could be used to fulfill demand elsewhere can be inefficient, resulting in new coin production costs that could have been avoided if coins held in inventory had been used instead to fulfill demand. To increase the efficiency of the Reserve Banks' process, CPO received approval from the Reserve Banks in October 2007 to centralize the development and placement of coin orders. Starting in three districts, CPO will determine the final numbers of circulated and new coins that will be shipped monthly to the Reserve Bank offices. CPO will also be responsible for ensuring that the offices maintain appropriate inventory levels. Results of a pilot program suggest that these changes could reduce inventories and smooth the U.S. Mint's production schedule. Federal Reserve and U.S. Mint officials generally agreed with the findings of the chapter and provided technical comments which were incorporated as appropriate.

BACKGROUND

One of the functions of the Reserve Banks is to fulfill the coin demand of the nation's depository institutions—which include commercial banks, savings and loan associations, and credit unions—by distributing coin inventories stored in the Reserve Banks' vaults and at coin terminals, including circulated coins and new coins ordered from the U.S. Mint. The Reserve Banks have 30 offices that provide coins to depository institutions and are responsible for an area within 1 of the Federal Reserve's 12 districts.[5] Figure 1 shows a map of the Reserve Bank districts (districts) and the locations of the offices that provide coin services.

As figure 2 shows, the Reserve Banks hold and distribute coins from their vaults and contract with armored carrier companies to hold the rest of the Reserve Banks' inventory.

As of December 31, 2007, 179 coin terminals held about 61 percent of the Reserve Banks' total coin inventory, in terms of volume. According to Reserve Bank officials, the arrangement between the Reserve Banks and the armored carrier companies that operate these coin terminals began because both parties agreed that having more distribution points would be more cost-efficient from a societal perspective. Federal Reserve officials and coin terminal operators said that, historically, this has been a "win-win" arrangement because it has eliminated the need for armored carriers to haul coins to and from the Reserve Banks before distributing them to the depository institutions. The armored carrier companies store Reserve Banks' coin inventory in their coin terminals at no charge. The agreement between the two entities (1) defines a limit on the value of inventory that a particular coin operator can hold for a Reserve Bank at a particular terminal and (2) requires the coin terminal operator to maintain liability insurance for loss of or damage to the Reserve Bank's coin inventory. The coin terminal agreements can be canceled with prior notice and without cause at any time by either party. The armored carrier companies also maintain depository institutions' coin inventories in the coin terminals at no charge; however, the companies earn revenue from the coin processing, wrapping, and transportation services that they provide to the depository institutions.

In addition to the coins held in their inventory, the Reserve Banks purchase new coins at face value from the U.S. Mint to fulfill depository institutions' demand.[6] To develop an annual production schedule and fulfill the Reserve Banks' coin orders, the U.S. Mint uses national coin demand forecasting models[7] to determine how many new coins to produce. U.S. Mint facilities in Philadelphia and Denver then produce the new coins, and the Mint ships the new coins to the Reserve Bank offices or coin terminals. Appendix II shows trends in the U.S. Mint's coin production data for fiscal years 2002 through 2007. The U.S. Mint also may transfer circulated coins between Reserve Bank offices. We discuss this matter in more detail later in the chapter.

Depository institutions order coins from the Reserve Banks to meet retailers' and the public's demand. These orders include requests for new commemorative circulating coins from congressionally enacted programs, such as the 50 State Quarters and the Presidential $1 Coins Programs, as well as for other coins for day-to-day transactional use.[8] Reserve Bank offices fill these orders with new and circulated coins held in the offices' vaults and at the coin terminals. Depository institutions contract with armored carriers to process and deliver the coins to them; then depository institutions provide coins to retailers and the general public. Depository institutions also return coins to the Reserve Banks when they have more coins in their inventory than they want to hold to meet demand. For example, when the public's demand for coins falls after the holiday season and the depository institutions have accumulated more coins than they want to hold for day-to-day transactions, the depository institutions deposit the extra coins with the Reserve Banks. According to two nationwide banking associations, the depository institutions have an incentive to limit the number of coins they hold in inventory because the institutions do not earn interest on coins held in their own vaults.

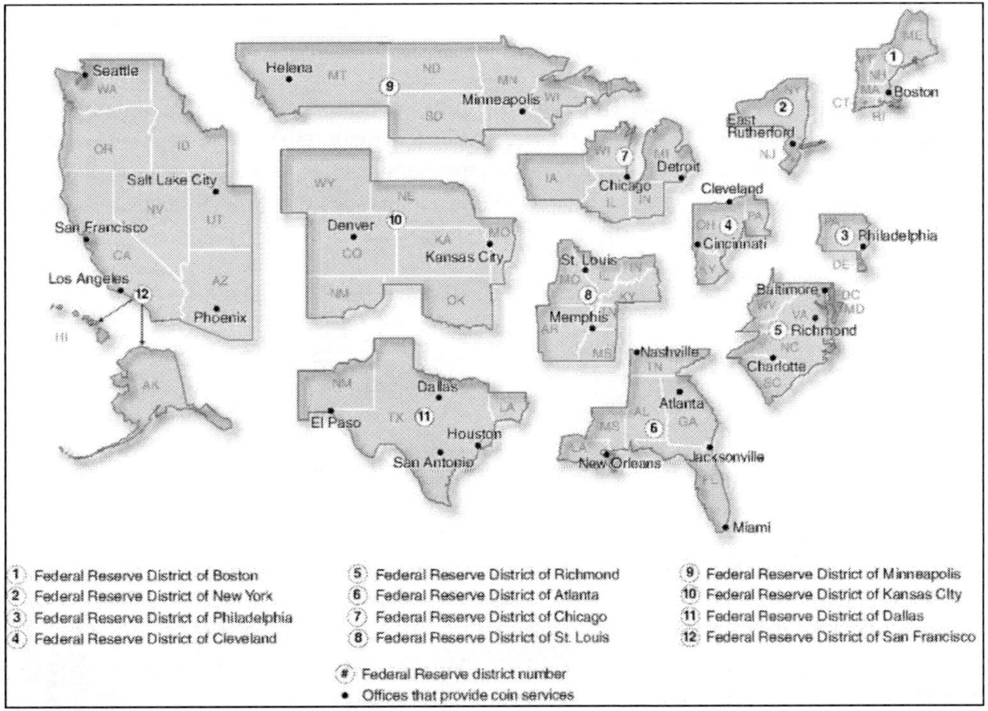

Sources: Federal Reserve (data) and Map Resources (map).

Note: The Phoenix and East Rutherford offices are processing centers that are responsible for distributing coins. The remaining 28 offices are Federal Reserve head offices and branches.

Figure 1. Map of Reserve Bank Districts and Locations of the Offices That Provide Coin Services.

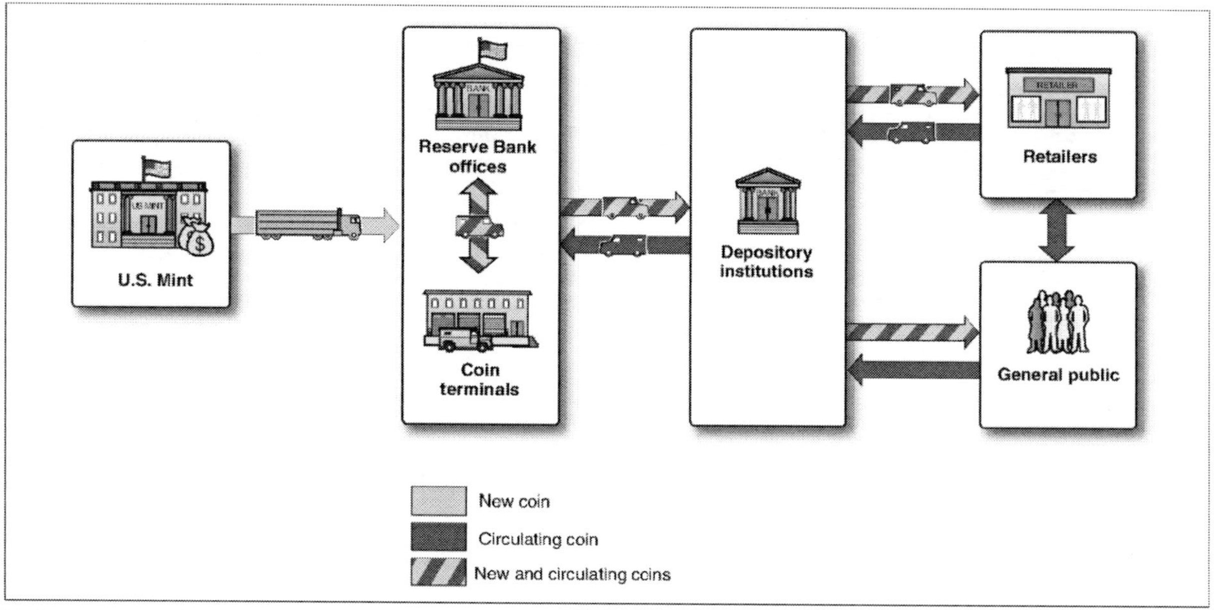

Source: GAO.

Notes: Some depository institutions choose not to receive coins directly from the Reserve Banks. Instead, these banks obtain coins through correspondent banks that have an account with a Reserve Bank. The term "retailers" encompasses any commercial business that uses coins, including retail stores, casinos, restaurants, and vending machine operators.

The new coins produced by the U.S. Mint are a small portion of the total number of coins in circulation. As we have previously mentioned, the U.S. Mint produced about $2 billion worth of coins in fiscal year 2007, while the total value of the coins in circulation was about $37 billion.

Figure 2. Coin Supply and Distribution Process.

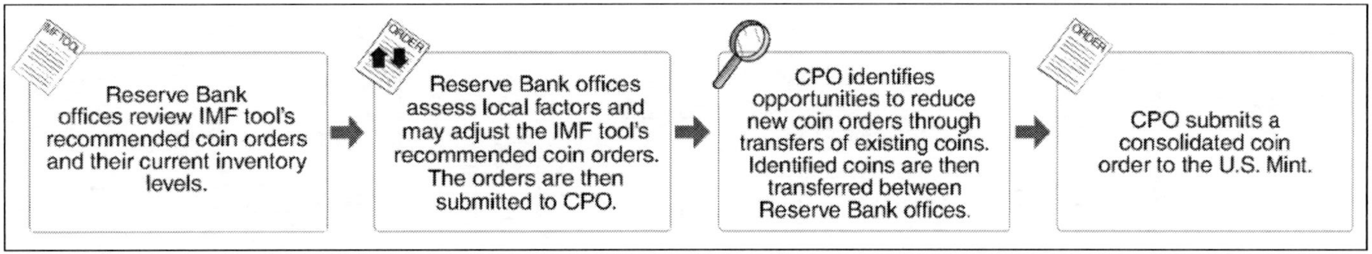

Source: GAO.

Figure 3. Reserve Banks' Current Monthly Coin Ordering Process.

THE RESERVE BANKS' PROCESS FOR ORDERING AND DISTRIBUTING COINS USES NEW COINS, COIN INVENTORIES, AND COIN TRANSFERS TO MEET DEMAND

The Reserve Banks' process for ordering and distributing coins uses orders of new coins from the U.S. Mint, the Reserve Bank offices' coin inventories, and transfers of circulated coins between Reserve Bank offices to meet estimates of depository institutions' demand. These estimates are based on coin demand forecasts generated by a forecasting tool. The offices prepare requests for coins on the basis of these estimates and on their own assessments of demand and send the requests to CPO for review. CPO then looks for opportunities to transfer circulated coins between Reserve Bank offices to help fulfill the offices' requests. CPO reduces the offices' requests for coins by the amounts of the transfers, consolidates the adjusted requests, and monthly sends a final consolidated order for new coins to the U.S. Mint.

Coin Demand Forecasts, Inventory Holdings, and Assessments of Local Market Demand Drive Reserve Bank Offices' Requests for New Coins

According to Federal Reserve officials, forecasting coin demand is not an exact science and requires judgment. Therefore, the Reserve Bank offices use both a data-driven process and professional judgment to develop coin orders. Specifically, the offices use an econometric inventory management and forecasting (IMF) tool that the Federal Reserve developed in consultation with the U.S. Mint to forecast coin demand at the Reserve Bank office level and to recommend coin orders for each office. The IMF tool analyzes historical data on coin payments to and receipts from depository institutions and is maintained by the Economic Research Group at the Federal Reserve Bank of San Francisco. According to documentation for the IMF tool, the tool is able to predict the seasonal fluctuations in coin demand fairly accurately because these fluctuations tend to be fairly regular. For example, the demand for coin rises in November in response to the public's demand for coins over the holidays and then decreases in January. While the timing of these fluctuations is fairly regular, their magnitude is more difficult to project, according to Federal Reserve officials. In addition, the IMF tool was developed about the same time that the commemorative circulating coin programs were beginning.

Therefore, according to Reserve Bank officials, the tool projects coin demand for economic transactions, but the tool does not estimate demand for collecting commemorative circulating coins. Hence, judgment is involved in estimating both the magnitude of seasonal fluctuations in coin demand and the demand for collecting commemorative circulating coins.

As shown in figure 3, currently, the 30 Reserve Bank offices receive data from the IMF tool each month as a starting point for preparing their coin orders. Most Reserve Bank officials told us that they start the monthly coin ordering process by examining the orders recommended by the IMF tool or their current inventory levels for each denomination.

Reserve Bank officials emphasized that although the IMF tool's analysis is a helpful starting point for the coin ordering process, assessments of local market factors are important because the tool's analysis is based on historical payments and receipts data and may not consider unique factors affecting future coin demand. Coin demand is affected by factors specific to particular districts. For example, five districts noted that local casinos were moving to coinless slot machines, which would reduce coin demand in and coin orders for these districts. Conversely, several districts increase their coin orders to account for collectors' demand when new coins are released for commemorative circulating coin programs, such as the 50 State Quarters Program. Reserve Bank officials noted that changes in the U.S. Postal Service's and local transit authorities' use of coins also affect coin demand. For example, in one district, the local transit authority retrofitted its ticket machines to dispense dollar coins, which resulted in greater demand for dollar coins in that district. Most of the districts cited coin recycling companies, such as Coinstar, as a factor affecting the number of coins returned by the depository institutions and the number of new coins to be ordered from the U.S. Mint. Coin recycling machines found in grocery stores, retail stores, and some depository institutions have made it easier now than it was in the past for the public to trade in coins for currency or some form of credit, such as a gift card. In some districts, coin recycling has returned large volumes of coins to circulation and to the Reserve Banks. Reserve Bank officials said that when more coins are returned than are ordered by the depository institutions, they reduce their orders of new coins from the U.S. Mint. According to data from one major coin recycling company, the value of coins returned to circulation through recycling grew from approximately $1 billion in 2000 to $2.6 billion in 2006.

To obtain information on local market factors, officials at the Reserve Bank offices talk with coin terminal operators and sometimes with officials at depository institutions in their districts. The coin terminal operators provide the Reserve Bank offices with daily inventory data on the Reserve Bank coins held by the terminals. The coin terminal operators hold inventory for both the depository institutions and the Reserve Banks and may provide the Reserve Banks with insight into changes in the depository institutions' coin demand. Some Reserve Bank officials also obtain information on coin demand through conversations with depository institution officials, usually in the course of discussing currency issues. During these conversations, the depository institutions can provide advance notice of any circumstances that may change coin demand, such as upcoming festivals or state fairs, which typically would increase their demand for coins. The conversations with coin terminal operators and depository institutions are important because officials at the Reserve Bank offices can obtain information on potential coin requests or deposits back with the Reserve Banks, which could affect the Reserve Banks' inventory levels or orders for new coins.

According to the Reserve Bank officials with whom we spoke, before the offices finalize and send their orders to CPO, they look for opportunities to transfer coins within their district to meet projected demand. For example, one Reserve Bank office may want additional coins, while another office may have more coins than it wants to hold to meet short-term demand. The Reserve Bank office works with the coin terminal operators to move the coins as needed. According to Reserve Bank and coin terminal officials, as part of their normal business, the coin terminal operators transport coins to and from the Reserve Banks and are able to absorb the costs of the transfers by combining them with previously scheduled pickups and deliveries for their depository institution customers.

CPO Coordinates the Reserve Banks' Coin Order and Identifies Opportunities for Reducing the Order through Transfers

In 2001, CPO began coordinating coin distribution from a national perspective on behalf of the Reserve Banks to enhance coordination with the U.S. Mint and look for opportunities to redistribute coin inventories. Historically, the Reserve Banks individually developed and submitted their own coin orders to the U.S. Mint without any insight into coin inventories in other districts or consideration of whether coins could be transferred from other districts to meet demand, rather than ordering new coins.[9] In 1999, shortages of pennies occurred in some regions of the country because some depository institutions were hoarding pennies and the U.S. Mint could not fulfill the Reserve Banks' increased orders for pennies. During this time, the Reserve Banks moved coins from one district to another to satisfy demand but did not have a centralized coordination process in place to facilitate these transfers, according to Federal Reserve officials. Following this experience, the Reserve Bank of San Francisco assumed responsibility for coordinating coin operations at Reserve Banks through its CPO. CPO is now the Reserve Banks' primary liaison with the U.S. Mint and is responsible for finalizing and submitting a monthly consolidated coin order for the Reserve Banks. According to Federal Reserve officials, CPO has focused on achieving system efficiencies by implementing more centralized coin management strategies, including enhancing coordination with the U.S. Mint; improving distribution channels by increasing the number of Reserve Bank coin terminals; and redistributing national inventories of coins, as appropriate, to meet demand, thereby reducing the need for new coins from the Mint.

With the exception of new releases of commemorative circulating coins, CPO determines whether the Reserve Banks' requests for coins can be filled with circulated coins in Reserve Banks' inventories or whether new coins need to be ordered from the U.S. Mint. CPO compares the Reserve Bank offices' requests for coins with the IMF tool's recommended orders and the offices' current inventory levels. According to CPO officials, if an office's request differs significantly from the order recommended by the IMF tool, CPO contacts the Reserve Bank office to discuss the reasons for the difference. CPO also compares current inventory levels with historic inventory data to determine whether the Reserve Banks have enough coins to meet seasonal changes in demand. While the Reserve Bank offices make the final decision on how many coins they request, a recent agreement will allow CPO, with input from the Reserve Bank offices, to make the final decision. We discuss this agreement in more detail later in the chapter.

CPO looks for opportunities to reduce the new coin order to the U.S. Mint by transferring coins from one district to another. CPO officials noted that using circulated inventory rather than purchasing new coins reduces the number of new coins that the U.S. Mint produces and the Mint's costs of production. Yet according to a U.S. Mint official, continuing demand for new coins means that using circulating inventory does not avoid the production of coins, but merely delays it. To determine whether coins can be transferred, CPO considers such things as constraints on storage space, the distance between the office or terminal that requests additional coins and the one that has available inventory, and insurance limits at the coin terminals. CPO then works with the U.S. Mint to transfer circulated coins between Federal Reserve offices that are more than 100 miles apart.[10] The U.S. Mint paid about $1.3 million for 638 coin transfers in fiscal year 2006 and about $915,000 for 404 coin transfers in fiscal year 2007.[11] According to U.S. Mint officials, the Mint contracts and pays for these coin transfers because balancing inventories among the Reserve Banks helps to lower the volatility of production for the Mint and the Mint has ongoing contracts for shipping large quantities of coins. However, according to a U.S. Mint official, the U.S. Mint is looking to phase out the practice of paying for transfers. The official recognizes that coin inventories may occasionally expand in some areas or regions, but believes that such conditions are temporary. Therefore, transferring coins from existing inventories may only temporarily delay the production of additional coins to meet the demands of commerce.[12] See appendix V for data on the number of transfers and the corresponding budget for fiscal years 2002 through 2007. Our analysis of Reserve Banks' order data shows that CPO reduced orders by about 10 percent in fiscal years 2006 and 2007 by fulfilling Reserve Bank offices' coin requests with circulated inventory. Specifically, the Reserve Banks submitted requests to CPO for approximately 18 billion coins in fiscal year 2006 and for approximately 16 billion coins in fiscal year 2007, and CPO was able to reduce these requests through transfers by over 2.2 billion coins in fiscal year 2006 and by over 1.5 billion coins in fiscal year 2007.

Once CPO makes adjustments and consolidates the Reserve Bank offices' orders, CPO submits a final new coin order to the U.S. Mint 1 month before the coins are scheduled to be delivered. The order includes a shipping schedule outlining when and where the coins should be shipped as well as a 5-month coin order forecast. Upon receiving the order from CPO, the U.S. Mint ensures that it will have the coins to fulfill the order and then distributes coins to the Reserve Banks and coin terminals from its production facilities in Philadelphia and Denver. Both U.S. Mint and Federal Reserve officials said that they continually communicate throughout the month on the coin order, and that the Reserve Banks have the flexibility to adjust the coin order and delivery destination.

CPO has several working groups of coin stakeholders, including depository institutions, vending machine operators, and armored carriers, to help address any potential or current coin distribution issues. For example, CPO interacts with depository institutions through its Customer Advisory Council, which currently consists of the 16 largest depository institutions in the country in terms of cash volume. Coins are typically not the primary focus of the council's meetings, but the meetings give the depository institutions an opportunity to discuss any concerns about coins, such as the distribution of newly released commemorative circulating coins. As mandated by law, the Secretary of the Treasury and the Federal Reserve's Board of Governors are taking steps to ensure that an adequate supply of dollar coins is available for commerce and collectors.[13] The U.S. Mint and the Federal Reserve are consulting with coin users and holding forums to identify stakeholders' ideas for the efficient distribution and circulation of dollar coins as well as other circulating coins.

THE RESERVE BANKS' PROCESS FULFILLS COIN DEMAND, BUT OPTIMAL INVENTORY RANGES ARE UNDEFINED

The Reserve Banks' process for ordering and distributing coins has fulfilled depository institutions' demand for the coins, but does not define optimal ranges for the Reserve Banks to hold in inventory to meet demand. Our analysis of Reserve Bank data showed that the Reserve Banks maintained enough inventory to meet demand, even when demand was greater than anticipated. Coin stakeholders confirmed that the Reserve Banks' process has fulfilled depository institutions' demand for coins in recent years. However, the Reserve Banks have taken a decentralized approach to inventory management that allows the Reserve Bank offices to use their own judgment to set inventory levels that they think are appropriate to meet future demand and avoid the risk of shortages. Reserve Bank officials expressed no concern about holding too many coins and told us that excess inventory is an issue only when coin inventories approach storage capacity limits. However, with rare exceptions, the Reserve Banks have more storage capacity than they need to maintain their current inventories, and, therefore, storage capacity does not serve as an incentive for the banks to evaluate and manage to optimal coin inventory ranges. To increase the efficiency of the distribution process, CPO has received approval from the Reserve Banks to centralize the development and placement of coin orders, and CPO will be responsible for ensuring that the offices maintain appropriate inventory levels.

The Reserve Banks' Ordering and Distribution Process Has Met Demand for Coins

The Reserve Banks' process has ensured that enough coins are available through orders of new coins and the Reserve Banks' inventories of circulated coins to meet the depository institutions' demand for coins. In each year since 1993, the number of coins demanded by the depository institutions has generally exceeded the number of coins deposited back to the Reserve Banks for all denominations, except the half-dollar. For example, as figure 4 shows, in fiscal year 2007, the Reserve Banks paid out 76 billion coins to the depository institutions (payments) and received 62 billion coins back from the depository institutions (receipts). This difference between payments and receipts is called "net pay." For example, net pay for fiscal year 2007 was about 14 billion coins. See appendix III for payments and receipts data, by denomination, for fiscal years 1993 through 2007.

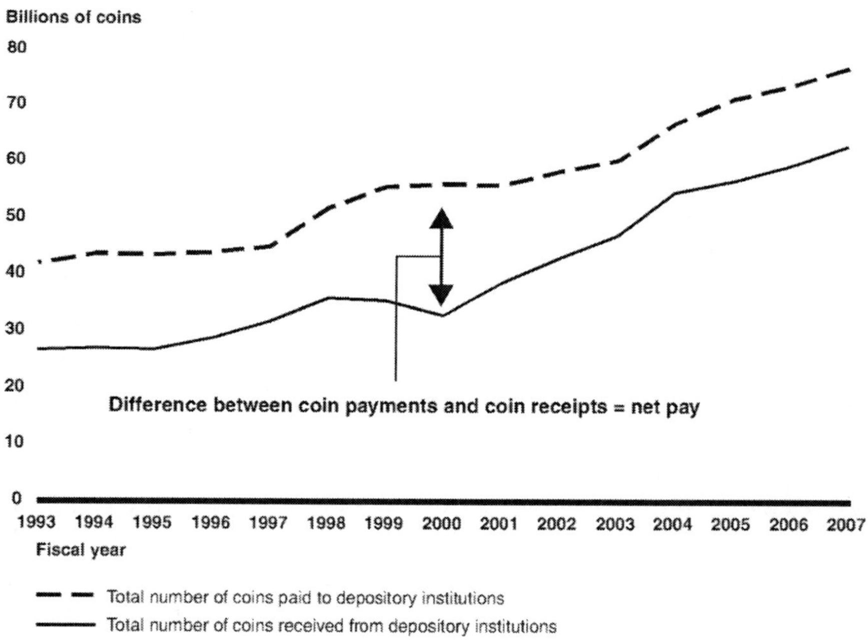

Source: Federal Reserve.

Figure 4. Number of Coins the Reserve Banks Paid to and Received from Depository Institutions, Fiscal Years 1993-2007.

Since the number of coins received by the Reserve Banks is less than the number of coins sent to the depository institutions to meet their demand, the Reserve Banks have to order new coins or use circulated inventory to meet demand. When depository institutions demand more coins than they return over a month or a year, net pay is positive for that period and additional coins have to be ordered or coin inventory has to be used to meet the demand. When depository institutions return more coins to the Reserve Banks than they order over a month or a year, net pay is negative for that period and the Reserve Banks' inventory of coins can grow. Net pay fluctuates throughout the year, depending on the public's spending patterns. Specifically, Reserve Bank data show that net pay was generally positive for all denominations, except the half-dollar, throughout the year, except in January when the demand for coins declines. Net pay for the half-dollar has been negative since fiscal year 2004 because the Reserve Banks received more half-dollars back than they paid out. Understanding and predicting net pay is critical to the Reserve Banks' ability to meet coin demand. According to Federal Reserve officials, net pay is positive for many reasons. For example, the public stores coins that it receives in jars and dresser drawers and sometimes discards coins. Collectors' demand for coins can also increase the Reserve Banks' payments for commemorative circulating coins, while limiting the Reserve Banks' receipts because the coins are kept out of circulation. When coins leave "active" circulation— that is, the coins are stored and not deposited or used for commerce—they are not available to meet depository institutions' demand.

During fiscal years 1993 through 2007, the Reserve Banks' aggregate orders for new coins tracked together with net pay fairly closely. For example, in fiscal year 2002, total orders for new coins—14.72 billion coins—were a little lower than the total net pay for all coins—15.11 billion coins—and resulted in a decrease in inventory for some denominations. In fiscal year 2007, total orders for new coins—14.63 billion coins—were a little higher than the total net pay for all coins—14.02 billion coins, suggesting the Reserve Banks ordered enough coins to fulfill net pay for the year and increased total inventory. Federal Reserve officials suggest that this aggregate annual increase of nearly 600 million coins can, in part, be explained by the introduction of the Presidential $1 Coin Program. After the first year of the program, the Reserve Banks report inventories of at least 300 million Presidential dollar coins. Orders for the penny constituted over half of the total orders for new coins. In fiscal year 2007, orders for the penny were 7.76 billion coins, while net pay was 7.79 billion coins. According to Reserve Bank officials, the difference between orders for new pennies and net pay resulted in an aggregate decline of about 30 million pennies in Reserve Banks' inventories.

The Reserve Banks strive to maintain sufficient inventories of coins to fulfill demand, despite seasonal and unanticipated changes and potential interruptions in the supply of new coins. First, inventory is important in handling the seasonal fluctuations in demand for coins. According to documentation on the IMF tool and Reserve Bank officials, this fluctuating demand can be met by either (1) adjusting the number of coins ordered to keep pace with known seasonal changes in demand or (2) keeping orders constant and allowing inventory to fluctuate in response to these changes in demand. The Reserve Banks place orders to keep the U.S. Mint's production schedule fairly consistent and allow inventories to fluctuate with the seasonality of coin demand. For example, Reserve Bank officials said they ensure that they have enough coins on hand to meet the high coin demand leading into the summer and holiday months. According to Federal Reserve officials, a Reserve Bank office may not transfer coins out of its area if the office knows that those coins will be needed in the next week or month. Federal Reserve officials also noted that although the Reserve Banks can predict the timing of seasonal changes in demand for coins, it is more difficult for them to predict the magnitude of the changes from one year to the next. Predicting demand is important because the U.S. Mint may not be able to produce enough coins within a short time frame to keep up with heavy demand.[14] Second, since there is some uncertainty in the actual demand for coins in any given month, the Reserve Banks' coin inventory provides a buffer against any changes in demand that may occur between the times the coins are ordered and received. Third, the Reserve Banks want to hold enough inventory to handle disruptions in supply from the U.S. Mint. For example, when the U.S. Mint's production facilities in Philadelphia shut down, starting in March 2002, for 7 weeks to correct safety concerns, the Mint worked with the Reserve Banks to ensure that coins were available to fulfill demand.

Figure 5 shows that when compared with expected demand, expressed as days of payable inventory, the Reserve Banks' overall inventory for the penny, nickel, dime, and quarter has generally decreased since fiscal year 2001.[15] For example, the penny inventory declined from an average of 32 days of payable inventory, or 3.0 billion coins, in fiscal year 2001 to an average of 16 days of payable inventory, or 2.2 billion coins, in fiscal year 2007. The nickel inventory declined from 37 days of payable inventory in fiscal year 2001 to 25 days of payable inventory in fiscal year 2007. Inventory levels throughout the year vary around these averages because of fluctuations in the public's spending patterns.

Figure 6 shows that the days of payable inventory for the half-dollar and dollar coins greatly exceed the levels for the other denominations and have generally increased in recent years. According to Federal Reserve officials, there is little demand for these denominations. Federal Reserve officials said that dollar coin inventories have also grown as a result of the Presidential $1 Coin Program, which requires the Federal Reserve to ensure that, during an introductory period, an adequate supply of each newly minted design (there are four new coins each year) is made available for commerce and collectors.

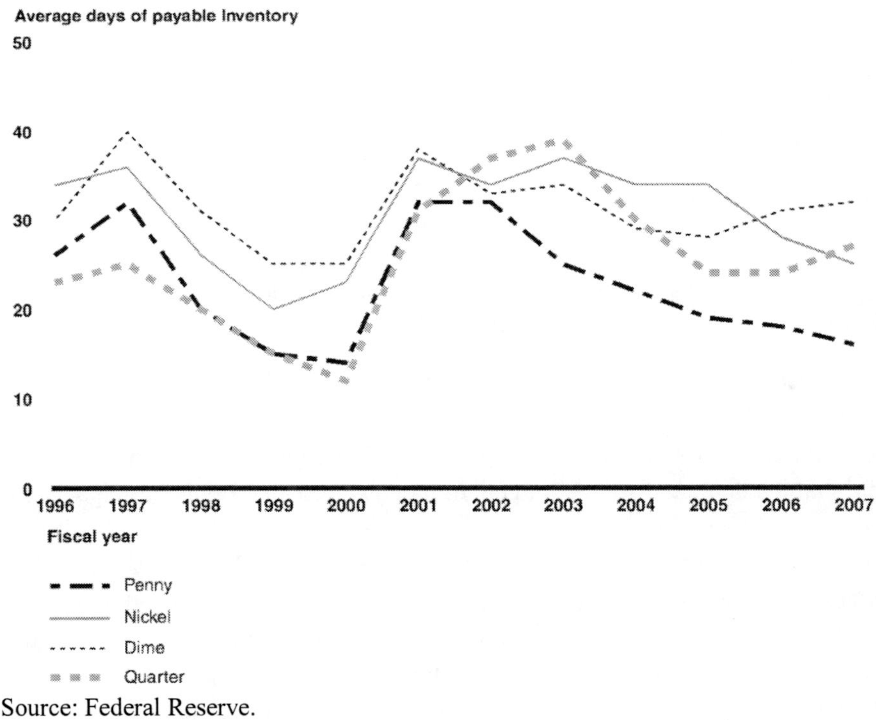

Source: Federal Reserve.

Note: The inventory data are represented in terms of average days of payable inventory. A day of payable inventory is the level of inventory needed by the Reserve Banks to meet 1 day's expected payments to depository institutions.

Figure 5. Average Days of Payable Inventory for the Reserve Banks for the Penny, Nickel, Dime, and Quarter, Fiscal Years 1996-2007.

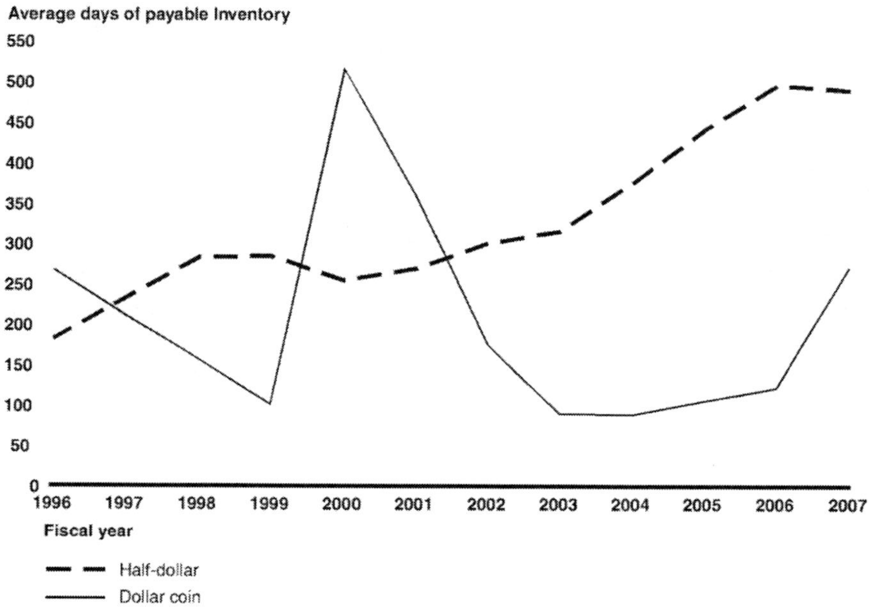

Source: Federal Reserve.

Figure 6. Average Days of Payable Inventory for the Reserve Banks for the Half-Dollar and Dollar Coin, Fiscal Years 1996-2007.

Several factors affected trends in the Reserve Banks' inventory levels during fiscal years 1993 through 2007. For example, inventory levels for all denominations dropped from fiscal years 1997 to 1999. Reserve Bank officials said that the demand for all coin denominations grew in 1999 in anticipation of the new millennium (Y2K). In fiscal year 2001, inventory levels for all denominations increased. According to the U.S. Mint's 2001 annual report, the economy, which is directly related to the demand for coins, took a downturn in the middle of fiscal year 2000, resulting in a decrease in coin demand and a buildup of coin inventories. According to Reserve Bank officials, the inventory trends for the quarter and dollar coin reflect the challenges posed by the commemorative circulating programs associated with these coins. The officials noted that commemorative circulating coin programs, such as the Presidential $1 Coin Program, create uncertainty about the demand for those denominations. These programs involve the distribution of multiple coin designs and require the Reserve Banks to order enough commemorative circulating coins to meet the normal demand for coins for commercial transactions as well as the potential demand from collectors when the coins are first introduced. According to Reserve Bank officials, the Reserve Banks did not initially have experience in working with commemorative circulating coins and placed large orders for state quarters to ensure that they would have enough on hand to meet both normal transactional demand and potential collector demand. As a result, more quarters flowed back to the Reserve Banks than Reserve Bank officials expected for the first several releases. Reserve Bank officials noted that their forecasts of demand for state quarters have improved, and that their inventory of quarters has declined. The officials also noted that even with more experience, however, programs, such as the Presidential $1 Coin Program, require the Reserve Banks to order more coins than they would otherwise use for transactional purposes, thereby increasing Reserve Banks' coin inventory levels beyond the levels they would ordinarily hold.

The coin terminal operators, banking associations, and Reserve Bank officials with whom we spoke confirmed that the Reserve Banks' process has fulfilled the depository institutions' demand for coins in recent years. Reserve Bank and CPO officials told us that they have been able to fill all depository institutions' requests for coin. The four coin terminal operators that we spoke with also noted that the Reserve Banks have been able to meet the demand of the depository institutions in their terminals. Finally, representatives from two banking associations said that constituent banks across the country have voiced no concern about the Reserve Banks' ability to distribute coins to the depository institutions.

Optimal Inventory Ranges Are Undefined, but the Reserve Banks Are Taking Steps to Manage Coin Inventory More Efficiently

The Reserve Banks have taken a decentralized approach to managing coin inventory, under which the Reserve Bank offices have decided what inventory levels are appropriate to keep on hand to meet forecasted demand and avoid the risk of coin shortages. Each Reserve Bank office has defined its own inventory levels on the basis of professional judgment and historical data, to meet demand and avoid running out of coins, and has used the capacity of its storage facilities as the key determinant of its maximum inventory levels. According to Reserve Bank officials, insurance limits at the coin terminals also help to define maximum inventory levels, but they can be adjusted, if necessary. Reserve Banks we spoke with had no specific levels for maximum inventory other than storage capacity and coin terminal insurance limits.

Because each Reserve Bank sets its own inventory levels, the districts manage to different inventory levels and hold varying levels of inventory relative to demand. For example, according to Reserve Bank officials, 3 of the 12 Reserve Banks generally try to hold at least 10 days of payable inventory for all denominations, while 6 of the 12 districts generally try to hold at least 20 or more days of payable inventory. Table 1 shows that for fiscal year 2007, the districts held varying levels of inventory relative to demand for the different denominations. For example, the penny inventories ranged from an average of 8 days in the Boston district to 26 days in the San Francisco district, while the quarter inventories ranged from 17 days in the St. Louis district to 40 days in the Philadelphia district.

Table 2 shows how the inventories for the penny, nickel, dime, and quarter have varied across Reserve Banks from fiscal years 1996 through 2007.[16]

Table 1. Average Days of Payable Inventory for the Penny, Nickel, Dime, and Quarter for the Reserve Banks, by District, in Fiscal Year 2007

Average days of payable inventory, fiscal year 2007				
District	**Penny**	**Nickel**	**Dime**	**Quarter**
Boston	8	16	20	19
New York	10	17	19	21
Chicago	13	19	27	29
Dallas	13	24	30	28
Cleveland	14	25	36	38
Kansas City	14	28	30	32
St. Louis	16	21	32	17
Philadelphia	17	23	25	40
Richmond	17	22	27	21
Atlanta	19	30	40	20
Minneapolis	23	41	42	33
San Francisco	26	35	44	31
Range across the Reserve Banks	**8 – 26**	**16 – 41**	**19 – 44**	**17 – 40**

Source: GAO analysis of Reserve Bank data.

Note: The inventory data are represented in terms of average days of payable inventory. A day of payable inventory is the level of inventory needed by the Reserve Banks to meet 1 day's expected payments to depository institutions.

Table 2. Range of Average Days of Payable Inventory for Penny, Nickel, Dime, and Quarter across Reserve Banks, Fiscal Years 1996-2007

Range of average days of payable inventory				
Fiscal year	**Penny**	**Nickel**	**Dime**	**Quarter**
1996	16 – 33	18 – 49	19 – 66	14 – 68
1997	21 – 52	22 – 50	17 – 101	10 – 137
1998	12 – 34	20 – 34	22 – 45	9 – 132
1999	8 – 24	13 – 31	16 – 42	9 – 55
2000	7 – 22	9 – 43	8 – 39	5 – 17
2001	20 – 49	26 – 64	26 – 60	23 – 51
2002	20 – 46	22 – 54	20 – 51	27 – 57
2003	16 – 40	25 – 61	24 – 63	16 – 78
2004	17 – 37	26 – 51	21 – 51	14 – 68
2005	13 – 32	25 – 50	18 – 42	11 – 55
2006	11 – 28	22 – 40	22 – 43	18 – 33
2007	8 – 26	16 – 41	19 – 44	17 – 40

Source: GAO analysis of Reserve Bank data.

Note: The inventory data are represented in terms of average days of payable inventory. A day of payable inventory is the level of inventory needed by the Reserve Banks to meet 1 day's expected payments to depository institutions.

According to Federal Reserve officials and documentation of the Reserve Banks' IMF tool, the districts hold varying levels of inventory relative to demand because of the differences in the variability in coin demand and because some offices have more storage capacity. To be able to respond to the variability in demand, some Reserve Bank offices need to hold more coins than other offices relative to demand to ensure that they have enough coins to meet demand at all times. See appendix IV for the inventory levels relative to demand, by district and denomination, for fiscal years 2005 through 2007.

Most Reserve Bank officials said that they were generally comfortable with their current inventory levels and expressed no concerns about having too many coins. Several Reserve Bank officials told us that they ordered conservatively—that is, they erred, if at all, on the side of ordering too many coins—because they were more concerned about not having enough coins to meet depository institutions' demand during high demand periods than about having too many coins at other times. CPO officials said it would be easier to deplete coin inventories than to build them up. Furthermore, most Reserve Bank officials were not concerned about having too many coins because they said they have ample on-site and off- site storage capacity and insurance levels at the coin terminals to store their coin inventory. For example, two districts have new, on-site coin vaults that were built within the last 10 years and were designed to accommodate the entire coin inventory for the district, even without coin terminals. Reserve Bank officials said that if the coin inventory level at a particular location approaches the storage limits, they work to move coins to another Reserve Bank or terminal.

CPO and Reserve Bank officials noted that the risk of not meeting depository institutions' demand for coins far exceeds the risk of having too many coins in inventory, as long as storage capacity exists. For example, Federal Reserve officials told us that in 1999, they had problems fulfilling the depository institutions' demand for pennies. During this time, the U.S. Mint could not produce enough pennies to fill Reserve Banks' orders. In addition, the Reserve Banks were not yet coordinating coin distribution nationally and, therefore, could not easily identify sources of inventory available for redistribution. According to Federal Reserve officials and coin terminal operators, some depository institutions became concerned that coins would not be available to meet their demand and began hoarding coins, which further exacerbated the problem. Federal Reserve officials noted that since 2001, CPO has coordinated Reserve Bank coin distribution from a national perspective to help ensure confidence in the availability of coins, and, since that time, the Reserve Banks have experienced no shortages.

Although we only heard about storage capacity concerns from Reserve Bank officials in one district, some coin terminal operators expressed concerns about coin inventory levels in their terminals. Officials from one Reserve Bank told us that, on rare occasions, they have had to negotiate with depository institutions on when the Reserve Bank could accept coin deposits because storage space was not immediately available. Reserve Bank officials also said that every effort is made to redistribute coins before insurance levels are reached at the coin terminals, and that the Reserve Bank offices work with the coin terminal operators to stay under the insurance limits. However, two of the four coin terminal operators with whom we spoke said that the Reserve Banks maintain higher inventory levels than the operators consider sufficient to respond to changes in demand. CPO and Reserve Bank officials said that they were sensitive to the numbers of coins being held at the coin terminals, but the officials noted that the Reserve Banks work to stay within the limits established in their agreements with the operators. One coin terminal operator noted that it did not have concerns about the Reserve Banks' coin inventory levels or the distribution process. However, this operator noted that high volumes of coin recycling activity posed a challenge in some of its terminals. This operator also said that CPO was helping to move some of the coins out of the terminals, but that the high volumes would continue to be a problem until coin stakeholders—coin terminal operators, depository institutions, and CPO—find a solution to equitably redistribute the recycled coins.

Although we recognize the importance of minimizing the risk of not having sufficient coins to meet demand at all times, the Reserve Banks' current approach to inventory management does not define an optimal range of inventory for the offices to meet demand. Inventory levels that greatly exceed likely future demand could result in the overproduction of new coins and in potential storage concerns for the coin terminal operators. Data show that the Reserve Banks' overall inventory levels relative to demand for all denominations, except the half-dollar and the dollar coins, have generally decreased since 2001. However, the Reserve Banks and coin terminals have sufficient capacity for the Reserve Banks to hold higher levels of inventory for some denominations than are likely to be used to meet demand. Moreover, the storage capacity at the coin terminals is provided to the Reserve Banks at no charge. As a result, the Reserve Banks lack an incentive to evaluate and manage to optimal coin inventory ranges. In addition, the current approach to inventory management could lead to the overproduction of new coins in the short term or to the retention in some districts of coin inventory that could be redistributed to meet demand in another district. Thus, a Reserve Bank may incur few or no charges for storing high inventory levels, but the U.S. Mint may incur costs for producing new coins when circulated coins may be available to fulfill demand.[17] Producing new pennies and nickels when circulated coins could be used instead is particularly inefficient, since these denominations cost more to produce than they are worth. According to Federal Reserve officials, to mitigate this risk, CPO has been working with the Reserve Banks to manage inventories from a national perspective by transferring, where appropriate, inventories from one Reserve Bank to another one. According to a U.S. Mint official, a continuing demand for new coins means that producing coins when there is production capacity is not a concern because these coins will eventually be needed. In fact, he indicated that delaying production when there is production capacity may actually increase costs in the long run because production costs, like other costs, tend to increase over time.

CPO has recognized the importance of further centralizing and increasing the efficiency of the Reserve Banks' approach to coin inventory management and has identified opportunities for doing so. In 2006, the Reserve Banks and the U.S. Mint co-chartered a 6-month pilot of a new inventory management approach in one district. During the pilot, CPO (1) managed the inventory using vendor software that forecasts coin demand at the Reserve Bank office or terminal level[18] to provide consistent upper and lower bounds for inventory levels at each terminal site in the district and (2) used this information to maintain inventory levels to meet demand in the district. The Reserve Bank office was then responsible for moving coins among the coin terminals to meet demand. The Reserve Banks and the U.S. Mint assessed the results of the pilot and found that the new approach reduced the risk of shortages, transportation expenses, and inefficiencies associated with the U.S. Mint' s production volatility as well as increased stakeholders' confidence in the coin distribution system. According to CPO officials, the pilot also demonstrated that the district's inventory levels could be reduced. As a result of the pilot, CPO received approval from the Reserve Banks in October 2007 to implement a more centralized approach to managing coin orders and inventories.[19] According to CPO officials, they are expecting to phase in this new approach, beginning with three districts in the second quarter of 2008.

When the new approach is implemented, CPO will have the final authority to determine orders on behalf of the Reserve Bank offices and will be responsible for managing inventory levels that are maintained at the office level. According to CPO officials, CPO will continue to provide the Reserve Bank offices with a recommended monthly order. The Reserve Bank offices will be able to review this order and suggest revisions, but ultimately CPO will decide on the final order for each office. Although Reserve Bank officials told us that under the current approach, their adjustments to the IMF tool's recommended coin orders were minimal, over the past 3 years the combined impact of these adjustments was sometimes substantial. For example, the IMF tool recommended a total order of $52 million in pennies for all of the Reserve Bank offices in fiscal year 2007. Following the offices' assessment of local market factors and the availability of transfers of circulated coins to fulfill the offices' requests, CPO submitted a total order of $77.6 million for new pennies to the U.S. Mint. CPO's ability to now decide on the number of coins each district will receive monthly could potentially result in decreased orders for new coins from the U.S. Mint. CPO is considering establishing inventory ranges for the Reserve Bank offices on the basis of factors such as historical trends in coin payments and receipts, the amount of time taken to transport coins to a Reserve Bank office, and storage capacity limits to better define the level of inventory to be held to meet demand. We believe that the establishment of inventory ranges could help CPO and the Reserve Banks evaluate and report on the effectiveness of CPO's inventory management approach. CPO officials believe that these changes will improve the Reserve Banks' inventory management because CPO can provide a national perspective on where inventory can be used to meet demand, including where coins can be moved when necessary to meet demand in one district, while freeing space for coin deposits in storage facilities that are approaching capacity in another district. U.S. Mint officials said that the new approach could allow the U.S. Mint to further smooth its production schedule, thereby lowering costs associated with unpredictable changes in production.

AGENCY COMMENTS

We provided a draft of this chapter to the Board of Governors of the Federal Reserve System and to the Department of the Treasury for their review and comment. The Director of the Division of Reserve Bank Operations and Payment Systems provided written comments. Overall, the Federal Reserve agrees with the findings in our report and believes that the data in the chapter reflect the Reserve Banks' efficient and effective management of coin inventories. The Federal Reserve also provided technical comments, which we have addressed in this chapter as appropriate. The Acting Deputy Director of the U.S. Mint provided oral comments stating that the agency agrees with the information in this chapter as it pertains to the U.S. Mint and provided technical comments, which we have also incorporated as appropriate.

Susan A. Fleming
Director, Physical Infrastructure Issues

APPENDIX I. OBJECTIVES, SCOPE, AND METHODOLOGY

The objectives of this chapter were to examine (1) the Reserve Banks' process for ordering and distributing coins and (2) the extent to which this process meets the depository institutions' demand for coins.

To describe the Reserve Banks' process for supplying coins throughout the country, we obtained and reviewed relevant articles, reports, economic studies, and technical documentation on how the Reserve Banks and the U.S. Mint determine the number of coins to be produced and distributed. We also interviewed Federal Reserve and U.S. Mint economists who were involved in the development of economic models used to predict coin demand. During these interviews, we reviewed how the national coin forecast models are used by both the Reserve Banks and the U.S. Mint and discussed the accuracy of these models in predicting net pay at the national level. We interviewed officials from the Federal Reserve's Board of Governors (Board), each of the 12 Reserve Bank districts, and the national Cash Product Office (CPO) to determine how coin orders are developed and submitted to the U.S. Mint. In addition, we reviewed statutes related to the Federal Reserve and U.S. Mint.

We also interviewed key stakeholders, including officials from the U.S. Mint, operators of coin terminals with agreements to store Reserve Bank coin inventory, and representatives of banking associations, to determine how the Reserve Banks work in collaboration with others to identify and fulfill the depository institutions' requests for coins. We obtained and analyzed information on the costs paid by the U.S. Mint to transport existing coins and analyzed the number of transfers between Reserve Bank districts since fiscal year 2002. To determine how CPO was able to reduce orders for new coins through transfers of existing coin inventory, we reviewed Reserve Bank data documenting actual coin demand and compared these data with the Reserve Banks' actual order to the U.S. Mint for new coins and the number of circulated coin transfers processed by CPO.

To determine the extent to which the Reserve Banks' coin distribution process meets the depository institutions' demand for coins throughout the country, we obtained data on the Reserve Banks coin payments to depository institutions, receipts for coins deposited by the depository institutions, orders for new coins, and inventory levels for fiscal years 1993 through 2007 for each coin denomination and for each Reserve Bank. We analyzed these data using Excel and SAS statistical analysis software. To calculate Reserve Banks' number of coins paid to the depository institutions and Reserve Banks' number of coins received from the depository institutions at the national and district level for all coin denominations, we converted the data from value of coins to volume of coins and then calculated fiscal year totals for each denomination at the national and district level. We created line charts to compare the total number of coins that Reserve Bank paid to depository institutions with the total number of coins that the Reserve Bank received from the depository institutions. To calculate net pay and the Reserve Banks' coin order to the U.S. Mint, we converted the data from value of coins to volume of coins and calculated fiscal year totals at the national and district level. We created line charts to compare the net pay data with the Reserve Banks' coin order data.

To calculate the Reserve Banks' days of payable inventory, we consulted with officials at the Board and CPO to determine an appropriate methodology. CPO and Reserve Banks calculate payable inventory information several different ways, depending upon what they are assessing. For the purposes of our review, we determined that a comparison of inventory relative to a 3-month daily average of payments for 3 years was the most appropriate calculation to determine the Reserve Banks' inventory position, because it compares inventory relative to what the Reserve Banks could reasonably have expected coin payments to be in the future. This methodology captures coin inventory levels relative to what Reserve Banks expected to need to meet future payments to depository institutions. For the numerator, we used end-of-month inventory levels for a given month. For the denominator, for the 3 previous years, we used the quarter following the inventory month used in the numerator to assess inventory levels relative to demand in the following quarter. For example, when we calculated days of payable inventory for December 2006, we used data for January, February, and March, 2004; January, February, and March, 2005; and January, February, and March, 2006, in the denominator. To calculate the average daily payment rate, we took the monthly payments data from each month of the quarter from the previous 3 years and divided by 21 business days to obtain an average daily payment rate for each month. We then totaled the daily payment rates for the 9 months and divided by 9 to obtain an average payment rate of the 3 quarters for the 3 years. To calculate the annual average days of payable inventory, by denomination, for each Reserve Bank, we averaged the monthly figures on days of payable inventory that we computed as we have previously described. Because of the methodology we used to calculate days of payable inventory, 1996 is the earliest year for which we can present the data. We used statistical analysis software to complete this analysis for each coin denomination at the national and Reserve Bank level.

We also interviewed officials at the Board and Reserve Banks to discuss factors affecting trends in the data, the level of inventory that each district tries to hold, and the Reserve Banks' approach to coin inventory management. To describe the Reserve Banks' new centralized approach to coin inventory management and how it might address concerns about inventory management, we interviewed officials at CPO and the Board about a 2006 pilot to test a new inventory management approach at the Reserve Bank of Cleveland.

To assess the reliability of the coin data we received from the Reserve Banks and U.S. Mint, we talked with agency officials about data quality control procedures and reviewed relevant documentation. For example, we reviewed audit reports for fiscal years 2006 and 2007 prepared by the Department of the Treasury's Office of Inspector General, which reported that the U.S. Mint's data were accurately presented and in conformity with generally accepted accounting principles. The U.S. Mint has received approximately 15 consecutive unqualified opinions. These internal control audits found no material weaknesses and found that the U.S. Mint is in compliance with the Federal Manager's Financial Integrity Act. For the Federal Reserve data, we reviewed an independent auditor's reports on the Federal Reserve's financial statements for fiscal years 1995 through 2006, and found that the Federal Reserve's data were accurately presented and in conformity with generally accepted accounting principles. We also performed advanced electronic testing to assess the reliability of the computer-processed data, and determined that these data were accurate, complete, and consistent and, therefore, sufficiently reliable for the purposes of this chapter.

We conducted this performance audit from April 2007 through March 2008 in accordance with generally accepted government auditing standards. Those standards require that we plan and perform the audit to obtain sufficient, appropriate evidence to provide a reasonable basis for our findings and conclusions based on our audit objectives. We believe that the evidence obtained provides a reasonable basis for our findings and conclusions based on our audit objectives.

APPENDIX II. COIN PRODUCTION TRENDS, BY DENOMINATION

Figures 7 through 13 show trends in the U.S. Mint's coin production data for fiscal years 2002 through 2007. These data represent all of the "circulating" coins produced by the U.S. Mint; they do not include the "proof" or "uncirculated" quality coins produced by the Mint.

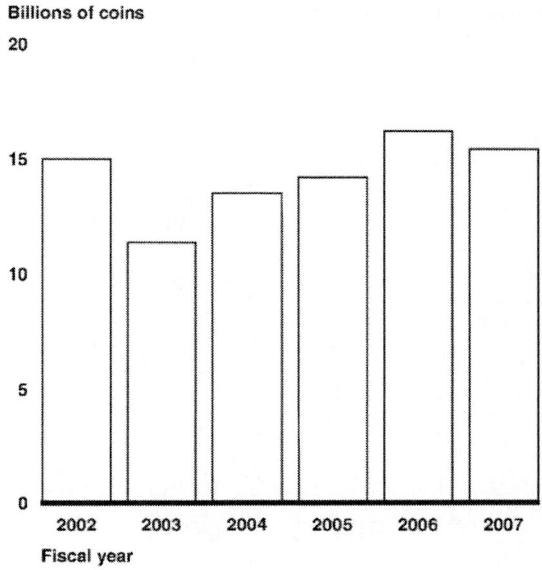

Source: U.S. Mint.

Figure 7. U.S. Mint's Coin Production for Fiscal Years 2002-2007, Total Coins (Penny, Nickel, Dime, Quarter, Half-Dollar, and Dollar).

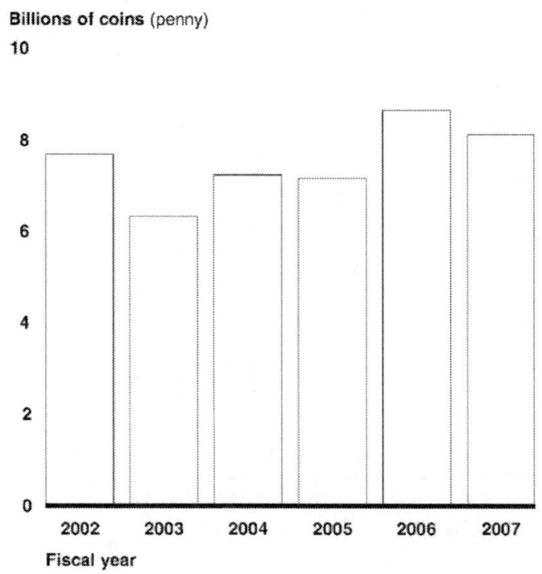

Source: U.S. Mint.

Figure 8. U.S. Mint's Coin Production for Fiscal Years 2002-2007, Penny.

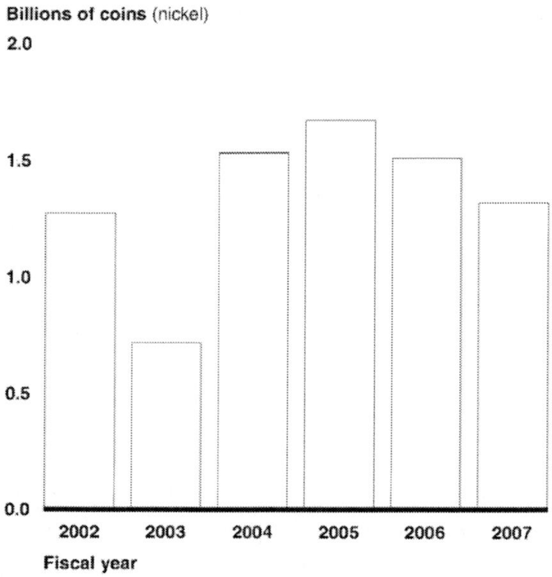

Source: U.S. Mint.

Figure 9. U.S. Mint's Coin Production for Fiscal Years 2002-2007, Nickel.

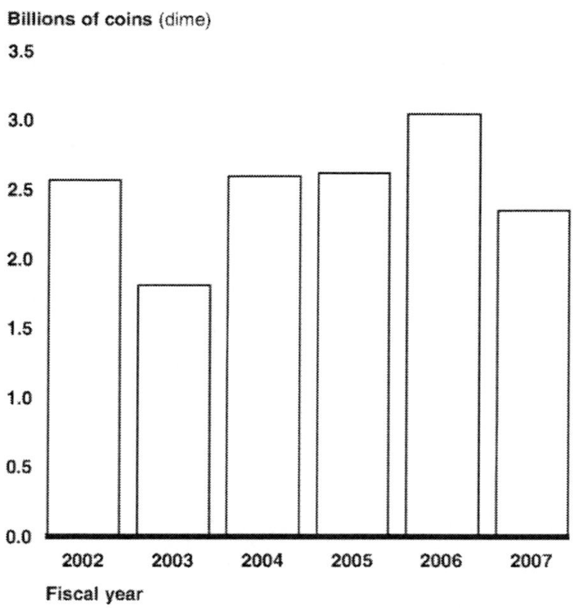

Source: U.S. Mint.

Figure 10. U.S. Mint's Coin Production for Fiscal Years 2002-2007, Dime.

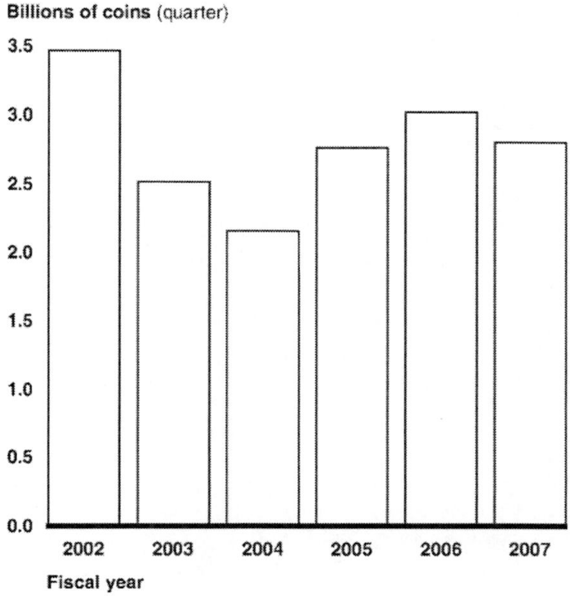

Source: U.S. Mint.

Figure 11. U.S. Mint's Coin Production for Fiscal Years 2002-2007, Quarter.

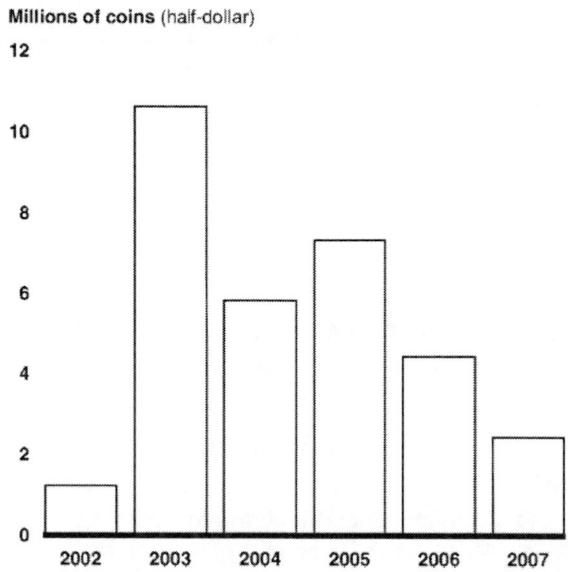

Source: U.S. Mint.

Figure 12. U.S. Mint's Coin Production for Fiscal Years 2002-2007, Half-Dollar.

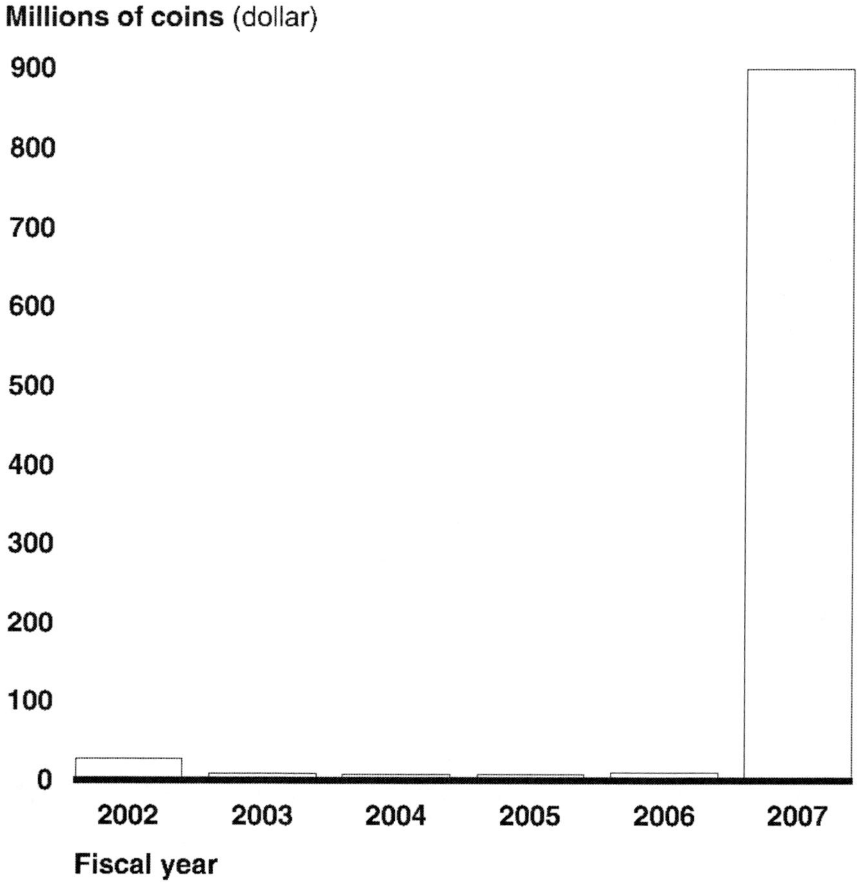

Source: U.S. Mint.

Figure 13. U.S. Mint's Coin Production for Fiscal Years 2002-2007, Dollar Coin.

APPENDIX III: NATIONAL PAYMENTS AND RECEIPTS DATA, BY DENOMINATION

The Reserve Banks make coin payments to depository institutions and accept coin deposits from depository institutions on a daily basis. Figures 14 through 19 show total payments and receipts for each coin denomination for all 12 Reserve Banks for fiscal years 1993 through 2007.

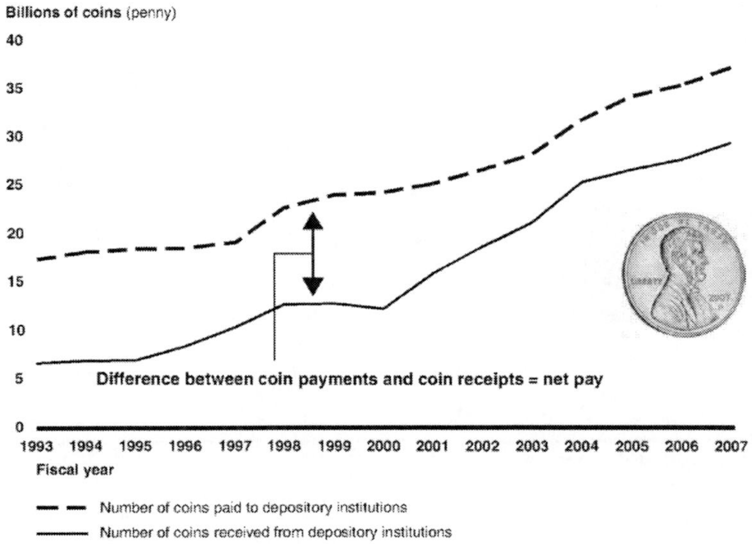

Sources: Federal Reserve and U.S. Mint.

Figure 14. Number of Pennies the Reserve Banks Paid to and Received from Depository Institutions, Fiscal Years 1993-2007.

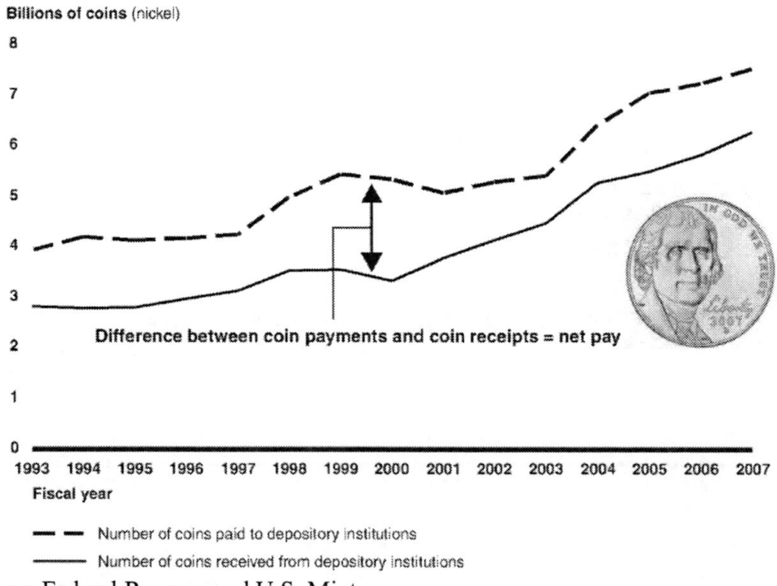

Sources: Federal Reserve and U.S. Mint.

Figure 15. Number of Nickels the Reserve Banks Paid to and Received from Depository Institutions, Fiscal Years 1993-2007.

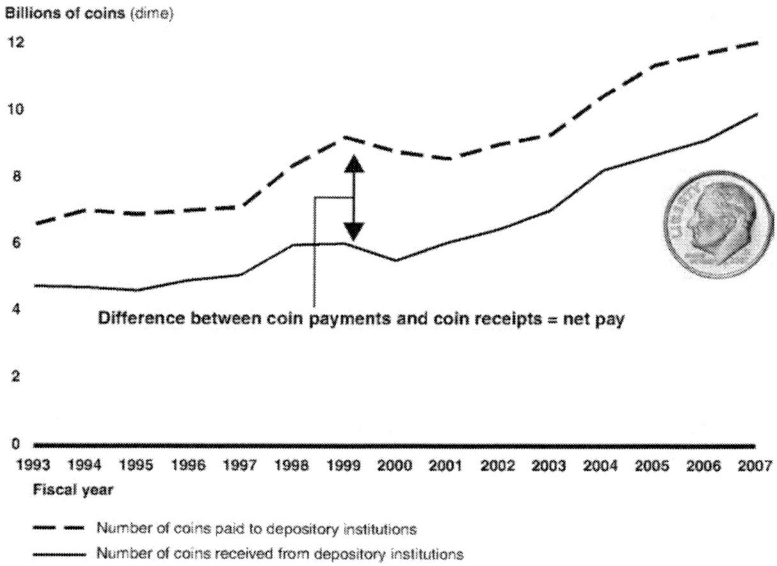

Sources: Federal Reserve and U.S. Mint.

Figure 16. Number of Dimes the Reserve Banks Paid to and Received from Depository Institutions, Fiscal Years 1993-2007.

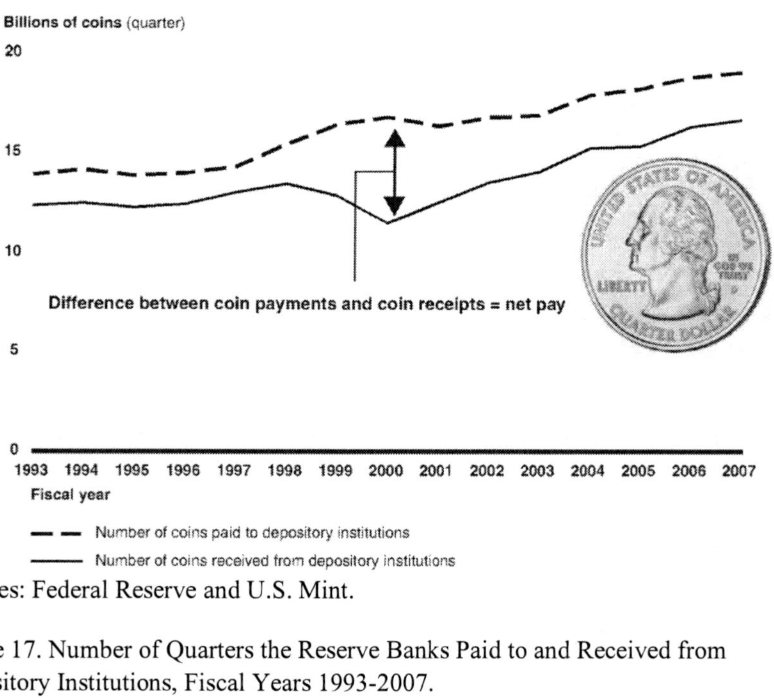

Sources: Federal Reserve and U.S. Mint.

Figure 17. Number of Quarters the Reserve Banks Paid to and Received from Depository Institutions, Fiscal Years 1993-2007.

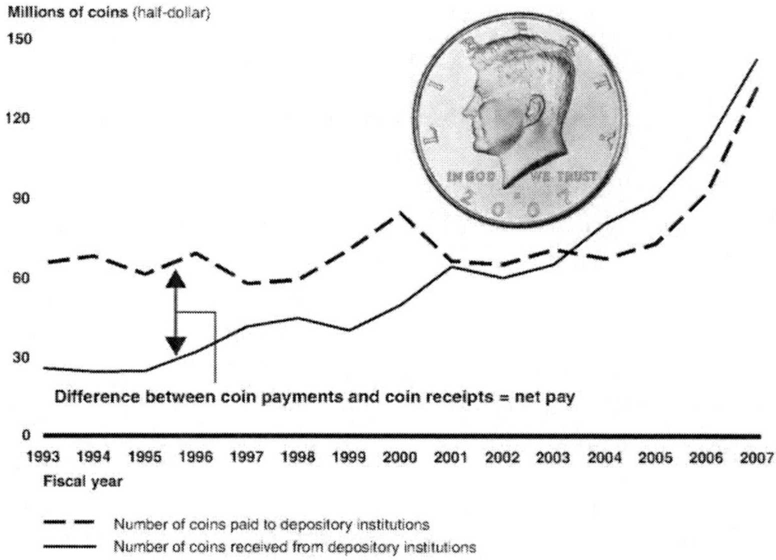

Sources: Federal Reserve and U.S. Mint.

Figure 18. Number of Half-Dollars the Reserve Banks Paid to and Received from Depository Institutions, Fiscal Years 1993-2007.

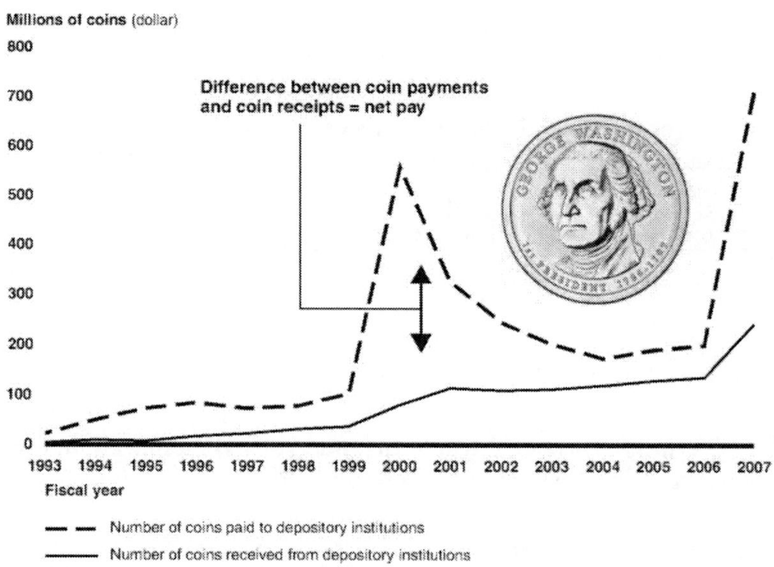

Sources: Federal Reserve and U.S. Mint.

Figure 19. Number of Dollar Coins the Reserve Banks Paid to and Received from Depository Institutions, Fiscal Years 1993-2007.

APPENDIX IV. AVERAGE DAYS OF PAYABLE COIN INVENTORY, BY RESERVE BANK DISTRICT AND COIN DENOMINATION

The Reserve Banks strive to maintain sufficient inventories of coins to fulfill demand, despite seasonal and unanticipated changes in demand for coins and potential interruptions in the supply of new coins. Tables 3 through 14 show the days of payable inventory maintained at each of the 12 Reserve Banks from fiscal years 2005 through 2007. Payable inventory represents the amount of inventory needed to meet expected demand for coins and is calculated by comparing inventories with average payment data over a 3-month period for the preceding 3 years.

Table 3. Average Days of Payable Inventory, by Denomination, for the Reserve Bank District of Boston, Fiscal Years 2005-2007

Fiscal year	Penny	Nickel	Dime	Quarter	Half-dollar	Dollar
2005	20	28	18	11	1,044	217
2006	17	29	35	27	1,087	181
2007	8	16	20	19	1,268	446

Source: GAO analysis of Federal Reserve data.

Table 4. Average Days of Payable Inventory, by Denomination, for the Reserve Bank District of New York, Fiscal Years 2005-2007

Fiscal year	Penny	Nickel	Dime	Quarter	Half-dollar	Dollar
2005	20	48	29	16	1,682	49
2006	11	25	22	18	1,745	87
2007	10	17	19	21	1,573	84

Source: GAO analysis of Federal Reserve data.

Table 5. Average Days of Payable Inventory, by Denomination, for the Reserve Bank District of Philadelphia, Fiscal Years 2005-2007

Fiscal year	Penny	Nickel	Dime	Quarter	Half-dollar	Dollar
2005	25	27	25	55	1,026	118
2006	23	27	29	33	1,261	95
2007	17	23	25	40	1,180	344

Source: GAO analysis of Federal Reserve data.

Table 6. Average Days of Payable Inventory, by Denomination, for the Reserve Bank District of Cleveland, Fiscal Years 2005-2007

Fiscal year	Penny	Nickel	Dime	Quarter	Half-dollar	Dollar
2005	17	46	30	25	551	115
2006	15	33	34	33	695	155
2007	14	25	36	38	771	490

Source: GAO analysis of Federal Reserve data.

Table 7. Average Days of Payable Inventory, by Denomination, for the Reserve Bank District of Richmond, Fiscal Years 2005-2007

Fiscal year	Penny	Nickel	Dime	Quarter	Half-dollar	Dollar
2005	19	29	19	15	538	119
2006	17	24	22	19	582	124
2007	17	22	27	21	550	355

Source: GAO analysis of Federal Reserve data.

Table 8. Average Days of Payable Inventory, by Denomination, for the Reserve Bank District of Atlanta, Fiscal Years 2005-2007

Fiscal year	Penny	Nickel	Dime	Quarter	Half-dollar	Dollar
2005	16	25	25	20	390	103
2006	19	27	34	19	549	152
2007	19	30	40	20	612	264

Source: GAO analysis of Federal Reserve data.

Table 9. Average Days of Payable Inventory, by Denomination, for the Reserve Bank District of Chicago, Fiscal Years 2005-2007

Fiscal year	Penny	Nickel	Dime	Quarter	Half-dollar	Dollar
2005	16	26	32	34	338	67
2006	14	22	30	23	389	74
2007	13	19	27	29	399	200

Source: GAO analysis of Federal Reserve data.

Table 10. Average Days of Payable Inventory, by Denomination, for the Reserve Bank District of St. Louis, Fiscal Years 2005-2007

Fiscal year	Penny	Nickel	Dime	Quarter	Half-dollar	Dollar
2005	13	29	21	21	344	88
2006	17	27	28	20	547	100
2007	16	21	32	17	539	296

Source: GAO analysis of Federal Reserve data.

Table 11. Average Days of Payable Inventory, by Denomination, for the Reserve Bank District of Minneapolis, Fiscal Years 2005-2007

Fiscal year	Penny	Nickel	Dime	Quarter	Half-dollar	Dollar
2005	23	50	30	18	281	106
2006	20	40	43	27	215	174
2007	23	41	42	33	234	391

Source: GAO analysis of Federal Reserve data.

Table 12. Average Days of Payable Inventory, by Denomination, for the Reserve Bank District of Kansas City, Fiscal Years 2005-2007

Fiscal year	Penny	Nickel	Dime	Quarter	Half-dollar	Dollar
2005	18	38	27	21	288	100
2006	23	29	27	29	225	93
2007	14	28	30	32	208	237

Source: GAO analysis of Federal Reserve data.

Table 13. Average Days of Payable Inventory, by Denomination, for the Reserve Bank District of Dallas, Fiscal Years 2005-2007

Fiscal year	Penny	Nickel	Dime	Quarter	Half-dollar	Dollar
2005	13	32	27	30	530	177
2006	17	25	28	25	392	167
2007	13	24	30	28	250	441

Source: GAO analysis of Federal Reserve data.

Table 14. Average Days of Payable Inventory, by Denomination, for the Reserve Bank District of San Francisco, Fiscal Years 2005-2007

Fiscal year	Penny	Nickel	Dime	Quarter	Half-dollar	Dollar
2005	32	46	42	29	235	159
2006	28	37	42	29	229	164
2007	26	35	44	31	203	275

Source: GAO analysis of Federal Reserve data.

Appendix V. Number of Coin Transfers and Related Costs, Fiscal Years 2002-2007

CPO looks for opportunities to reduce orders for new coins to the U.S. Mint by transferring circulating coins from one Reserve Bank district to another. The U.S. Mint pays for the cost for transfers over 100 miles. Table 15 shows the number and cost of transfers paid by the U.S. Mint from fiscal years 2002 through 2007.

Table 15. U.S. Mint Coin Transfers and Cost Information, Fiscal Years 2002-2007

Fiscal year	Number of transfers	U.S. Mint transfer cost
2002	299	$479,707
2003	496	744,823
2004	640	1,239,128
2005	677	1,350,698
2006	638	1,273,481
2007	404	914,769

Source: U.S. Mint data.

End Notes

[1] The costs of producing other coins, such as the quarter and dollar coins, are below the face values of these coins. For example, in fiscal year 2007, the quarter cost the U.S. Mint 9.8 cents to produce and the dollar coin cost 15.7 cents, according to the Mint's annual report.

[2] Proposed legislation—Coin Modernization and Taxpayer Savings Act of 2008, H.R. 5512, 110th Cong. (2008); Coin Modernization and Taxpayer Savings Act of 2007, H.R. 3956, 110th Cong. (2007); and Coinage Materials Modernization Act of 2007, H.R. 3330, 110th

Cong. (2007)—would give the Secretary of the Treasury the authority to change the weight and content of circulating coins, which could reduce the U.S. Mint's production costs. Currently, the weight and composition of U.S. coins is set forth in law. See 31 U.S.C. § 5112.

3 Although one of the Reserve Banks' responsibilities is to ensure that enough coins and currency are available to meet depository institutions' demand, we discuss in this chapter only the coin services provided by the Reserve Banks.

4 The Reserve Bank data represent data for all 30 offices that provide coins to depository institutions.

5 The Reserve Banks and their offices also perform other functions and services unrelated to coins, such as supervising member banks and bank holding companies.

6 As we have previously mentioned, the production costs of most coins are below their face values. This difference between production cost and face value is called "seigniorage," or the profit earned by the U.S. government from making coins. Seigniorage reduces the government's requirement to borrow money from the public to finance the government's debt.

7 The forecasting models take into account several factors, including historical data on coin demand and economic variables, such as the inflation rate as measured in the Consumer Price Index and the federal funds rate, which is the interest rate that banks charge each other for overnight loans. According to U.S. Mint officials, until recently, the Mint averaged the results of five national coin demand forecasting models—two models maintained by the Mint and three models maintained by the Federal Reserve—to estimate demand and plan a long-term production schedule. In late 2007, the U.S. Mint stopped using its models and now uses only the three models supported by the Federal Reserve. According to U.S. Mint officials, they made this change as part of the Mint's efforts to increase the efficiency of its operations.

8 Depository institutions can order Presidential dollar coins directly from their Reserve Bank for a specified period of time before the public release date for the coin. This advance ordering helps the depository institutions to have the coins on hand on the public release date to meet their customers' demand.

9 The Reserve Banks are separate legal entities that, before 2001, managed their own coin inventories to meet demand within their districts. The Board exercises general supervision over the Reserve Banks.

10 The Reserve Banks pay for transfer between offices that are less than 100 miles apart.

11 According to 31 U.S.C. § 5136, all expenses incurred by the Secretary of the Treasury for operations and programs of the U.S. Mint that are determined to be ordinary and reasonable incidents of Mint operations and programs are authorized to be paid out of the U.S. Mint Public Enterprise Fund. The statute defines "Mint operations and programs" as the activities concerning and assets used in the distribution of coinage.

12 The official also noted that delaying production, when the U.S. Mint has production capacity, may actually increase costs in the long run because production costs, like other costs, tend to increase over time.

13 The Presidential $1 Coin Act of 2005, § p, 31 U.S.C. § 5112(p).

14 In fiscal year 2007, the U.S. Mint had an average cycle time of 61 days. The cycle time starts when the order for the raw materials is placed and ends when the coin order is filled.

15 The inventory data are represented in terms of days of payable inventory. A day of payable inventory is the level of inventory needed to meet 1 day's expected payments to depository institutions. See appendix I for additional information on this calculation.

16 Because of our methodology in calculating average days of payable inventory data, 1996 is the earliest year for which we can present the data. See appendix I for more details.

17 Even though the production costs of other coins are less than their face values, resulting in a financial gain to the government (called seigniorage), there are still societal costs associated with producing these coins, such as the metal resources used to make the coins.

[18] According to the Reserve Bank officials, the IMF tool forecasts coin demand for an area covered by the Reserve Bank office, which could include several coin terminals.

[19] The Federal Reserve has chosen in the past to manage payments services on a systemwide basis for reasons of efficiency and to ensure effective operations of Reserve Bank programs. For example, the Federal Reserve consolidated the management of some payment services, such as check clearing and direct deposits, provided by the individual Reserve Banks. Federal Reserve committees worked with payments industry officials to develop standards to facilitate increased use of electronic check processing and to foster technical change on the basis of the preference of most payment system participants. As a result of these efforts, the Federal Reserve was able to consolidate check processing operations and apply emerging technologies to the Reserve Banks' business processes that led to improvements in quality and a reduction in costs. See GAO, *Federal Reserve System: Update on GAO's 1996 Recommendations*, GAO-02-774 (Washington, D.C.: Sept. 25, 2002), for more information.

In: U.S. Circulating Coins
Editor: Catherine Solorio

ISBN: 978-1-63117-184-0

Chapter 3

THE UNITED STATES MINT AT A GLANCE*

United States Mint

UNITED STATES MINT (MINT)

The Mint is the world's largest coin manufacturer. Our men and women manufacture and distribute circulating coins, precious metal and collectible coins, and national medals to meet the needs of the United States. Our vision is to become the finest mint in the world, through excellence in our people, products, customer service, and workplace.

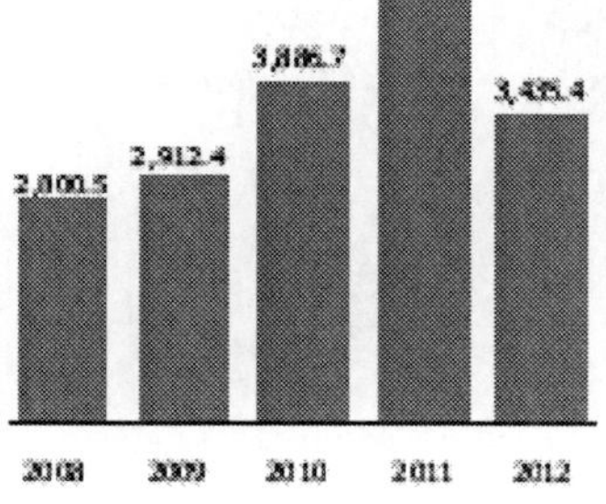

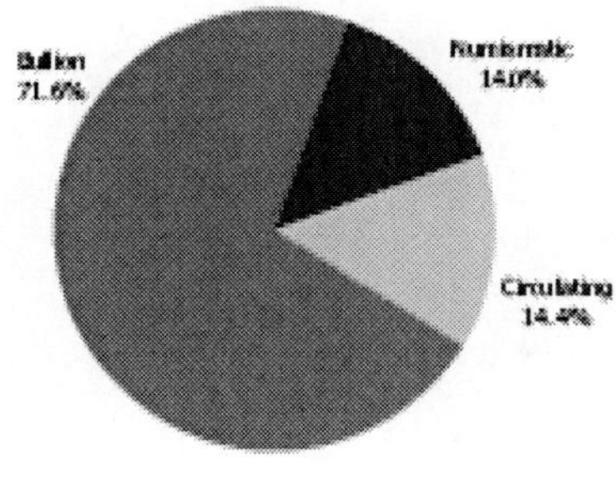

* This document is taken from the first section of the 2012 Annual Report of the United States Mint.

Circulating Coinage

The Mint is the sole manufacturer of legal tender coinage in the United States. The Mint's highest priority is to effciently and effectively mint and issue circulating coinage.

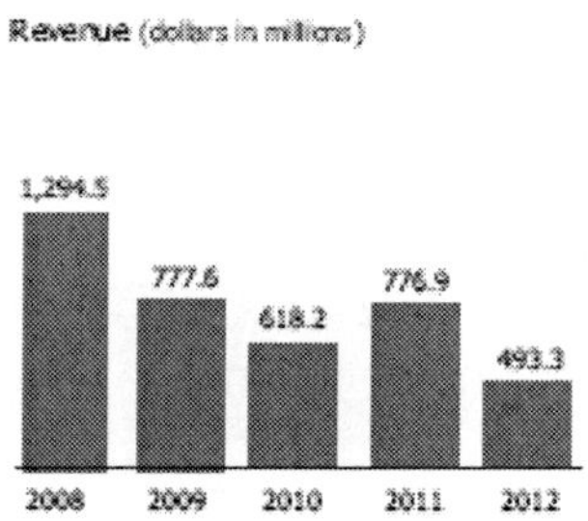

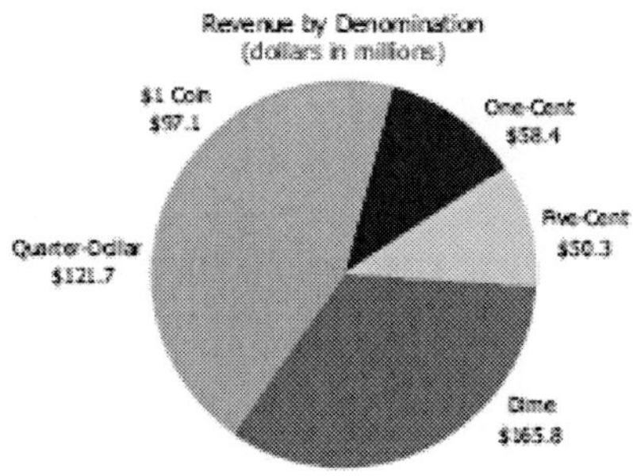

Bullion Coins

The Mint is the world's largest producer of gold and silver bullion coins. The bullion program provides consumers a simple and tangible means to acquire precious metal coins. Investors purchase bullion coins for the intrinsic metal value and the United States Government's guarantee of each coin's metal weight, content, and purity

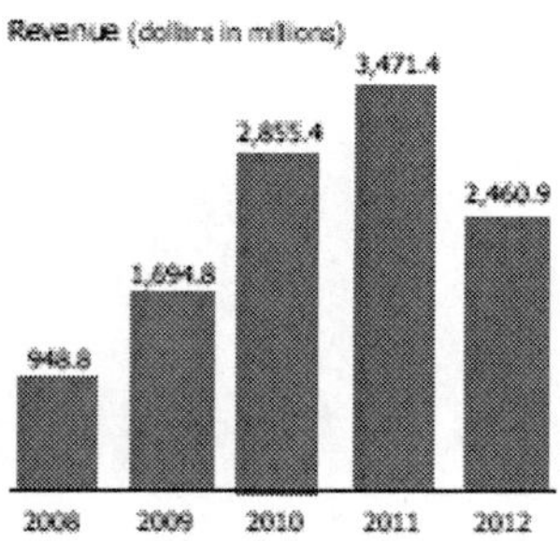

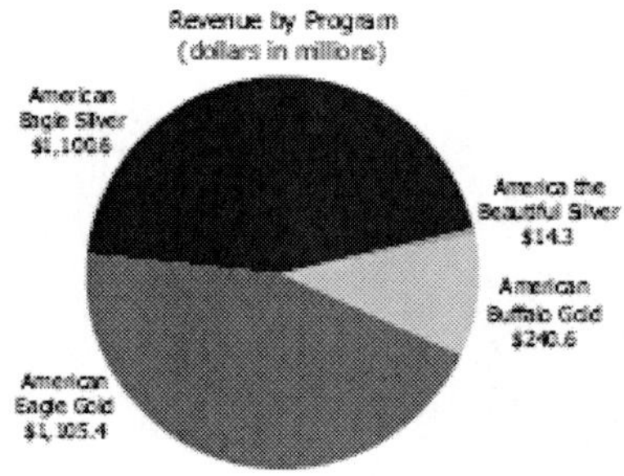

Numismatic Products

The Mint prepares and distributes numismatic products for collectors and those who desire high-quality versions of coinage. Most of our recurring products are required by federal statute. Others are required by individual public laws.

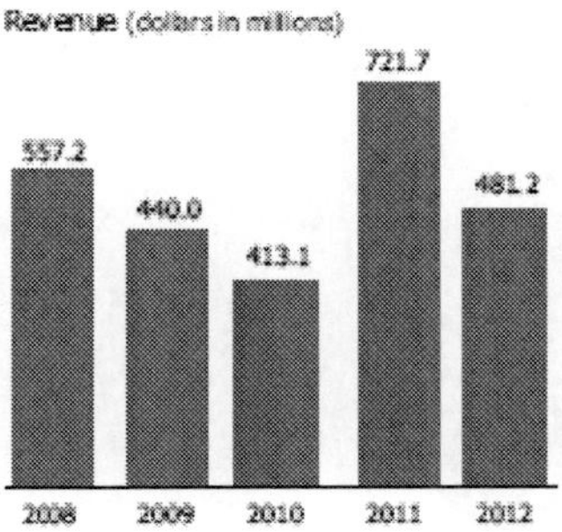

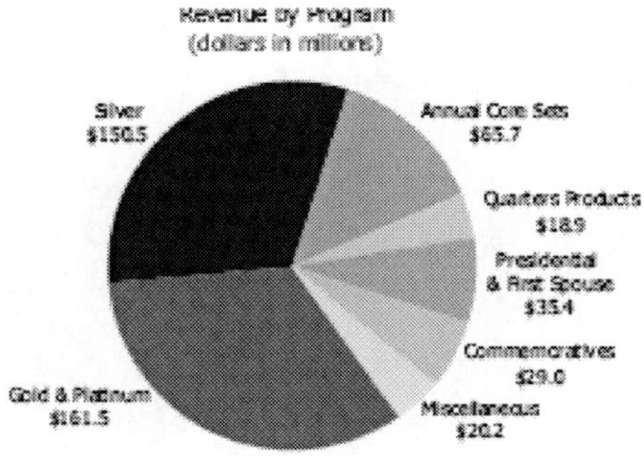

SEIGNIORAGE AND NET INCOME

Seigniorage is the difference between the face value and cost of producing circulating coinage. The Mint transfers seigniorage to the Treasury General Fund to help finance national debt. Net income from bullion and numismatic operations can also fund federal programs.

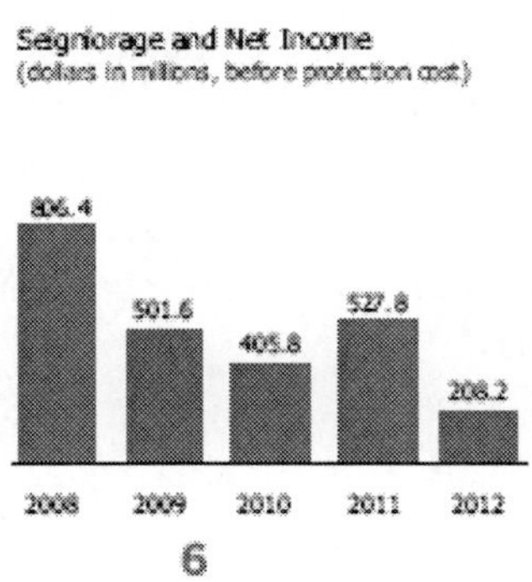

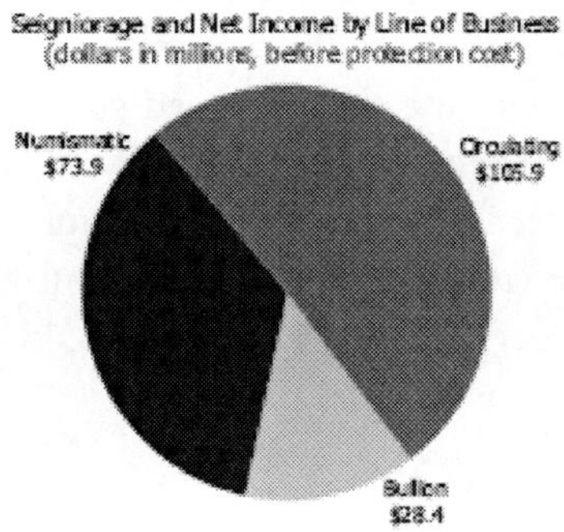

2012 PERFORMANCE

Revenue and net income was lower across all three business lines in FY 2012. Total revenue was $3,435.4 million, decreasing $1,534.6 from last year. Although circulating shipments increased 22.8 percent from last year, circulating revenue decreased. Selling, general and administrative (SG&A) expenses declined 4.6 percent from last year, and the cost of goods sold (COGS) decreased 28.2 percent to $3,079.5 million. Total seigniorage and net income, before Protection expenses, decreased 60.6 percent to $208.2 million compared to last year.

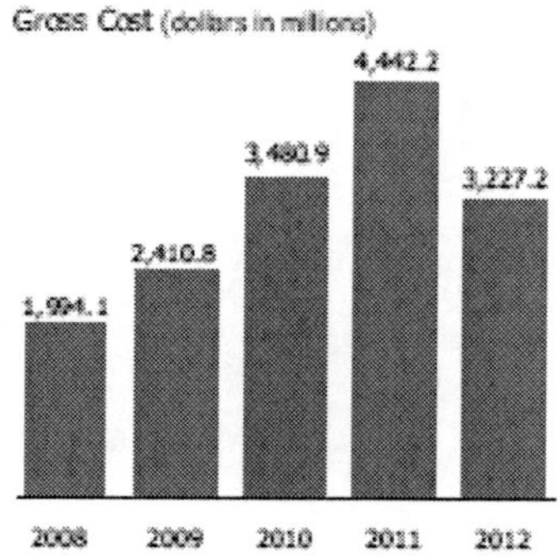

CIRCULATING COINAGE

Circulating coin shipments increased 22.8 percent to 9,082 million coins in FY 2012. Shipments of all coin denominations except $1 coins increased from FY 2011, with quarters experiencing the strongest annual percentage growth. Despite the increased shipments, circulating revenue and seigniorage decreased compared to last year because $1 coin shipments ceased in December 2011. Circulating revenue decreased 36.5 percent to $493.3 million. Seigniorage decreased 69.6 percent to $105.9 million. Seigniorage per dollar issued decreased to $0.21 from $0.45 last year.

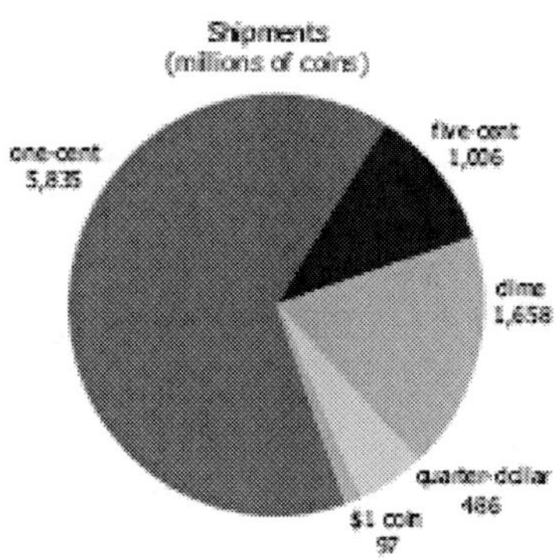

BULLION COINS

Demand for bullion coins slowed in FY 2012 after two years of unprecedented growth. The Mint sold 34.8 million ounces of gold and silver bullion coins in FY 2012, down 10.4 million ounces from last year. Total bullion revenue decreased 29.1 percent to nearly $2.5 billion in FY 2012, because gold bullion revenue decreased $551.4 million and silver revenue decreased $459.1 million compared to last year. Bullion net income decreased 56.8 percent to $28.4 million. Bullion net margin decreased to 1.2 percent compared to 1.9 percent last year.

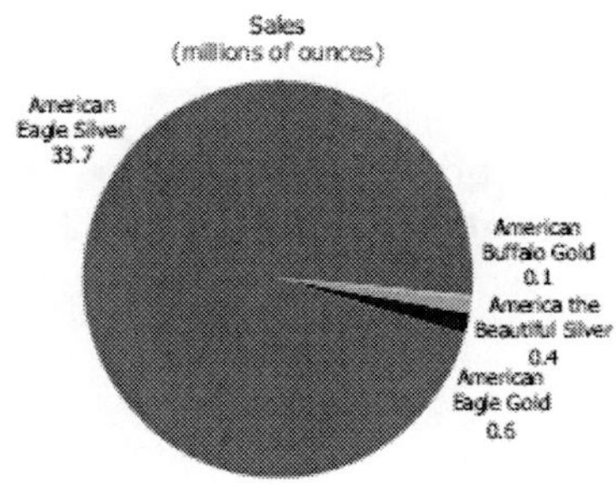

NUMISMATIC PRODUCTS

Numismatic sales decreased 23.3 percent to 5.6 million units in FY 2012. Numismatic revenues decreased 33.3 percent to $481.2 million mainly because of a decrease of $208.4 million in gold and platinum product revenue and a decrease of $41.7 million in annual core sets revenue. Numismatic net income decreased 34.7 percent to $73.9 million. Numismatic net margin decreased to 15.4 percent compared to 15.7 percent last year.

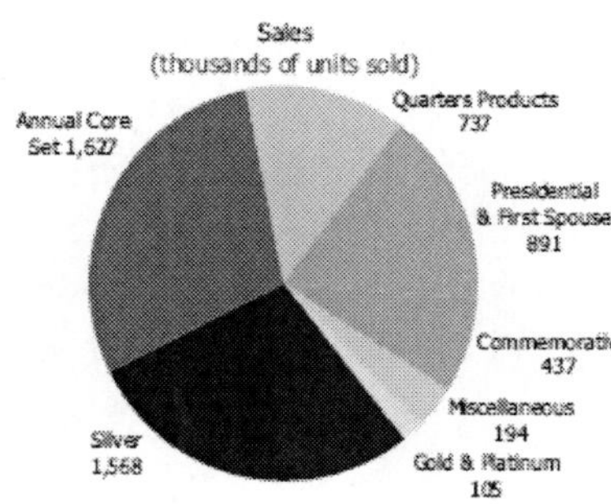

Transfer to the General Fund

In FY 2012, the Mint made an on-budget transfer of $77 million to the Treasury General Fund. This transfer consisted of FY 2011 numismatic and bullion program earnings after protection costs. The Mint made no off-budget transfers to the General Fund this fiscal year.

Instead, the Mint determined that all amounts in the PEF resulting from FRB receipts on the sale of circulating coins were required to mitigate the risks of future potential economic uncertainty, impacts to our circulating program from continued penny and nickel losses, and loss of revenue from the suspension of $1 coin production.

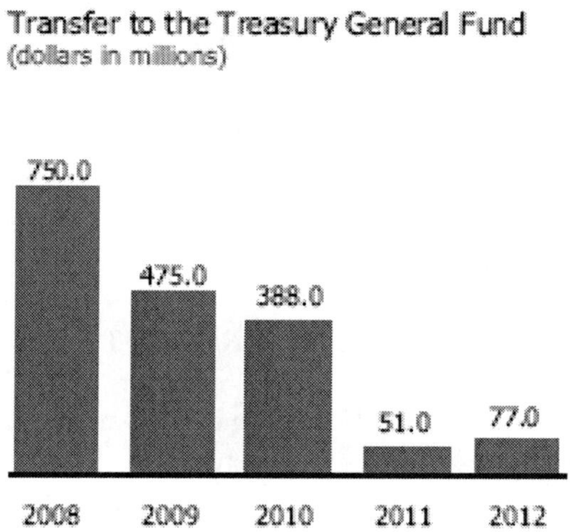

Meet The Nation's Need for Circulating Coins

As America's sole manufacturer of legal tender coinage, the efficient and effective production and distribution of coinage is the Mint's highest priority.

We mint and issue circulating coins to the FRB in quantities necessary to replenish inventory and fulfill the demand of commercial banks and other fi nancial institutions.

These financial institutions then distribute coins to meet the demand of retailers and the public. The Mint recognizes revenue from the sale of circulating coins at face value when they are shipped to the FRB.

Presidential $1 Coin Program Changes

Congress enacted the Presidential $1 Coin Act of 2005, which mandated the Mint issue four new Presidential $1 Coins each year beginning in 2007. As each coin was introduced, the FRB ordered enough to meet the initial demand of financial institutions. Demand for each new coin usually dropped soon after introduction and financial institutions ended up returning about 40 percent of the $1 coins to the FRB. By December 2011, the FRB vaults held more than 1.4 billion $1 coins.

Coins stored in FRB vaults do not function as a means of conducting commercial transactions and are not a prudent use of taxpayer resources. Therefore, in December 2011, the Secretary of the Treasury suspended minting Presidential $1 Coins for circulation.

The Mint continues to produce Presidential $1 Coins to meet public demand through the numismatic sales channel, as we do with the half-dollar coin.

Circulating Results

Demand for newly minted circulating coinage increased in FY 2012 compared with prior years.

However, the mix of coin denominations shipped to the FRB changed, lowering circulating revenue and seigniorage generated from operations. Compared to last year, shipments increased for all coin denominations except $1 coins.

The total number of circulating coins shipped to the FRB increased 22.8 percent to 9,082 million coins in FY 2012 from 7,396 million pieces in FY 2011.

Quarter shipments experienced the greatest annual growth, increasing 50.5 percent from FY 2011. Penny shipments were 64.2 percent of total shipments, up from 58.0 percent of total shipments in FY 2011.

Circulating (dollars in millions except seigniorage per $1 issued)

	2012	2011	2010	2009	2008	% Change 2011 to 2012
Value of Shipments	$ 493.3	$ 776.9	$ 618.2	$ 777.6	$ 1,294.5	(36.5%)
Gross Cost	$ 387.4	$ 428.1	$ 317.4	$ 349.8	$ 588.3	(9.5%)
Cost of Goods Sold	$ 325.8	$ 364.7	$ 239.2	$ 251.7	$ 491.3	(10.7%)
Selling, General & Administrative	$ 61.6	$ 63.4	$ 78.2	$ 98.1	$ 97.0	(2.8%)
Seigniorage	$ 105.9	$ 348.8	$ 300.8	$ 427.8	$ 706.2	(69.6%)
Seigniorage per $1 Issued	$ 0.21	$ 0.45	$ 0.49	$ 0.55	$ 0.55	

Shipments, Costs and Seigniorage by Denomination (coins and dollars in millions except seigniorage per $1 issued)

2012	One-Cent	Five-Cent	Dime	Quarter-Dollar	Half-Dollar	$1	Mutilated & Other	Total
Coins Shipments	5,835	1,006	1,658	486	–	97	–	9,082
Value of Shipments	$ 58.4	$ 50.3	$ 165.8	$ 121.7	$ –	$ 97.1	$ –	$ 493.3
Gross Cost	$ 116.4	$ 101.5	$ 82.7	$ 54.9	$ –	$ 20.5	$ 11.4	$ 387.4
Cost of Goods Sold	$ 96.5	$ 84.1	$ 69.5	$ 46.6	$ –	$ 17.7	$ 11.4	$ 325.8
Selling, General & Administrative	$ 19.9	$ 17.4	$ 13.2	$ 8.3	$ –	$ 2.8	$ –	$ 61.6
Seigniorage	$ (58.0)	$ (51.2)	$ 83.1	$ 66.8	$ –	$ 76.6	$ (11.4)	$ 105.9
Seigniorage per $1 Issued	$ (0.99)	$ (1.02)	$ 0.50	$ 0.55	$ –	$ 0.79	$ –	$ 0.21

2011	One-Cent	Five-Cent	Dime	Quarter-Dollar	Half-Dollar	$1	Mutilated & Other	Total
Coins Shipments	4,289	914	1,403	323	–	467	–	7,396
Value of Shipments	$ 42.9	$ 45.7	$ 140.3	$ 81.0	$ –	$ 467.0	$ –	$ 776.9
Gross Cost	$ 103.1	$ 102.2	$ 79.3	$ 36.0	$ –	$ 84.2	$ 23.3	$ 428.1
Cost of Goods Sold	$ 85.4	$ 86.1	$ 67.1	$ 30.3	$ –	$ 72.5	$ 23.3	$ 364.7
Selling, General & Administrative	$ 17.7	$ 16.1	$ 12.2	$ 5.7	$ –	$ 11.7	$ –	$ 63.4
Seigniorage	$ (60.2)	$ (56.5)	$ 61.0	$ 45.0	$ –	$ 382.8	$ (23.3)	$ 348.8
Seigniorage per $1 Issued	$ (1.40)	$ (1.24)	$ 0.43	$ 0.56	$ –	$ 0.82	$ –	$ 0.45

2010	One-Cent	Five-Cent	Dime	Quarter-Dollar	Half-Dollar	$1	Mutilated & Other	Total
Coins Shipments	3,487	359	887	252	–	414	–	5,399
Value of Shipments	$ 34.9	$ 17.9	$ 88.7	$ 63.2	$ –	$ 413.5	$ –	$ 618.2
Gross Cost	$ 62.3	$ 33.1	$ 50.6	$ 32.2	$ 0.1	$ 130.7	$ 8.4	$ 317.4
Cost of Goods Sold	$ 62.3	$ 33.1	$ 40.8	$ 24.6	$ 0.1	$ 69.9	$ 8.4	$ 239.2
Selling, General & Administrative	$ –	$ –	$ 9.8	$ 7.6	$ –	$ 60.8	$ –	$ 78.2
Seigniorage	$ (27.4)	$ (15.2)	$ 38.1	$ 31.0	$ (0.1)	$ 282.8	$ (8.4)	$ 300.8
Seigniorage per $1 Issued	$ (0.79)	$ (0.85)	$ 0.43	$ 0.49	$ –	$ 0.68	$ –	$ 0.49

COGS decreased 10.7 percent to $325.8 million in FY 2012 from $364.7 million in FY 2011. A component of this was a decrease in the market prices of copper, nickel, and zinc.

Average daily market prices for copper and zinc decreased 13.8 percent and 15.8 percent, respectively, from FY 2011 to FY 2012, while the average daily market price for nickel decreased 26 percent over the same time period. The Mint saved about $41 million in FY 2012 due to the decreased metal costs compared to last year.

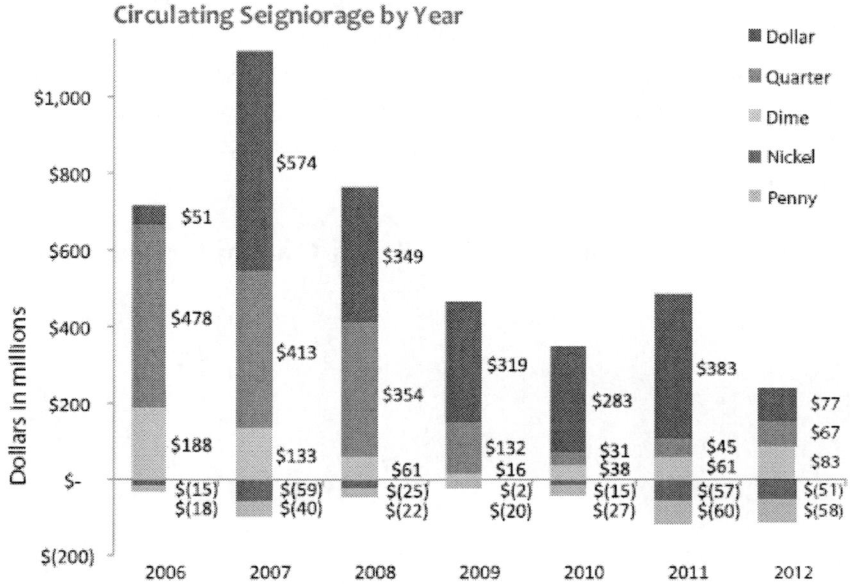

Shows seigniorage generated by denomination for the last seven years.

Apart from metals, plant expenses at Philadelphia and Denver decreased by about 3 percent, even though our circulating coinage shipments increased by 22.8 percent.

The Mint achieved this reduction largely due to decreased depreciation, salaries and beneßts, and energy expenses.

SG&A expenses decreased by 2.8 percent to $61.6 million in FY 2012 from $63.4 million in FY 2011.

This was primarily due to a 30.8 percent reduction in expenses for $1 coin programs and manufacturing administration. More SG&A expenses were absorbed by the penny, nickel, dime, and quarter coins because we suspended production of $1 coins for circulation.

FY 2012 unit costs decreased for all denominations compared to last year. The unit cost for both penny and nickel denominations remained above face value for the seventh consecutive ßscal year. Although there was higher demand for penny and nickel coins, lower unit costs generated a smaller FY 2012 loss ($109.2 million) for these denominations compared to FY 2011 ($116.7 million).

Unit Cost of Producing and Distributing Coins by Denomination

2012	One-Cent	Five-Cent	Dime	Quarter-Dollar	Half-Dollar	$1
Cost of Goods Sold	$ 0.0163	$ 0.0829	$ 0.0415	$ 0.0943	$ –	$ 0.1802
Selling, General & Administrative	$ 0.0034	$ 0.0173	$ 0.0080	$ 0.0171	$ –	$ 0.0288
Distribution to FRB	$ 0.0003	$ 0.0007	$ 0.0004	$ 0.0016	$ –	$ 0.0021
Total Unit Cost	$ 0.0200	$ 0.1009	$ 0.0499	$ 0.1130	$ –	$ 0.2111
2011	One-Cent	Five-Cent	Dime	Quarter-Dollar	Half-Dollar	$1
Cost of Goods Sold	$ 0.0197	$ 0.0938	$ 0.0474	$ 0.0923	$ –	$ 0.1531
Selling, General & Administrative	$ 0.0041	$ 0.0176	$ 0.0087	$ 0.0176	$ –	$ 0.0251
Distribution to FRB	$ 0.0003	$ 0.0004	$ 0.0004	$ 0.0015	$ –	$ 0.0021
Total Unit Cost	$ 0.0241	$ 0.1118	$ 0.0565	$ 0.1114	$ –	$ 0.1803
2010	One-Cent	Five-Cent	Dime	Quarter-Dollar	Half-Dollar	$1
Cost of Goods Sold	$ 0.0176	$ 0.0916	$ 0.0454	$ 0.0956	$ –	$ 0.1659
Selling, General & Administrative	$ –	$ –	$ 0.0110	$ 0.0302	$ –	$ 0.1469
Distribution to FRB	$ 0.0003	$ 0.0006	$ 0.0005	$ 0.0020	$ –	$ 0.0029
Total Unit Cost	$ 0.0179	$ 0.0922	$ 0.0569	$ 0.1278	$ –	$ 0.3157

Note: Before FY 2011, SG&A costs were allocated based on gross margin. Little or no allocated SG&A expense was applied to the penny or nickel, which generated negligible or negative gross margins. This policy changed to allocate SG&A expenses based on the costs to manufacture these products.

INDEX

A

B

C

G

H

I

J

L

M

N

O

P

Q

R

S